WITHDRAWN

Fabulous!

A LOVING, LUSCIOUS, AND LIGHTHEARTED LOOK AT FILM FROM THE GAY PERSPECTIVE

by Donald F. Reuter

BROADWAY BOOKS

NEW YORK

PRINTED IN THE UNITED STATES OF AMERICA

Library of Congress Cataloging-in-Publication Data
Reuter, Donald F.
Fabulous!: a loving, luscious, and lighthearted look at film from the gay perspective/
[written and designed by Donald F. Reuter].— 1st ed.
   p. cm.
Includes index.
ISBN 0-7679-1600-X (alk. paper)
1. Homosexuality and motion pictures. 2. Motion pictures—United States—Plots, themes, etc. I. Title.
PN1995.9.H55R48 2004
791.43'653—dc22   2003062775

First edition published 2004
10 9 8 7 6 5 4 3 2 1

Frontispiece, from top: Scene stills of *Suddenly, Last Summer* (Everett), *The Best of Everything* (Kobal), and *Valley of the Dolls* (Kobal). *Title spread, left:* Scene still from *The Wizard of Oz.* Everett. *Title spread, right:* Scene still of Barbra Streisand as Fanny Brice in *Funny Girl.* Everett. *This spread, left:* Judith Anderson as Mrs. Danvers in *Rebecca.* Kobal. *Right:* Scene still of *The Best of Everything,* featuring Hope Lange, Suzy Parker, and Joan Crawford. Kobal. *Following spread, left:* Publicity shot of the female cast of *Where the Boys Are,* featuring from the left, Paula Prentiss, Dolores Hart, Yvette Mimieux, and Connie Francis. Everett. *Following spread, right:* Scene still of Mark Wahlberg in *Boogie Nights.* Kobal. (For more movie details, see Index for page references.)

AA and AAN refer to Academy Award and Academy Award Nomination.

Contents

In Preview! — 8

★

Coming Attractions! — 11

★

Now Showing! — 25
Seventy-five "fabulous!" films

Adam's Rib — 28

Airport — 31

All About Eve — 32

Auntie Mame — 35

Babe — 36

The Bad and the Beautiful — 39

The Bad Seed — 40

Bagdad Café — 43

Barefoot in the Park — 44

The Best of Everything — 47

Billy Elliot — 48

The Birds — 51

Boogie Nights — 52

Breakfast at Tiffany's — 55

Breaking Away — 56

The Bride of Frankenstein — 59

Cabaret — 60

Can't Stop the Music — 63

Carrie — 64

Chicago — 67

Clueless — 68

Cobra Woman — 71

Dangerous Liaisons — 72

Dinner at Eight — 75

Doctor Zhivago — 76

Double Indemnity — 79

Dumbo — 80

Ed Wood — 83

Election — 84

The Fly — 87

Funny Girl — 88

The Ghost and Mrs Muir — 91

The Heiress — 92

The Hours — 95

How to Marry a Millionaire — 96

Imitation of Life (1959) — 99

L.A. Confidential — 100

Laura — 103

Law of Desire (La Ley del Deseo) — 104

Mahogany — 107

Mildred Pierce — 108

Mommie Dearest — 111

Moonstruck — 112

Mr. Blandings Builds His Dream House — 115

Murder on the Orient Express — 116

My Fair Lady — 119

North by Northwest — 120

Now, Voyager — 123

The Oscar — 124

The Philadelphia Story — 127

Pillow Talk — 128

Polyester — 131

The Red Shoes — 132

Risky Business — 135

A Room with a View — 136

Rosemary's Baby — 139

Sabrina (1954) — 140

Shanghai Express — 143

Sitting Pretty — 144

Some Like It Hot — 147

The Sound of Music — 148

A Star Is Born (1954) — 151

Suddenly, Last Summer — 152

Sunset Boulevard — 155

The Ten Commandments (1956) — 156

That's Entertainment! — 159

Thelma and Louise — 160

The Thin Man — 163

Valley of the Dolls — 164

The Way We Were — 167

What Ever Happened to Baby Jane? — 168

Where the Boys Are — 171

The Wizard of Oz — 172

The Women — 175

Young Frankenstein — 176

★

Also Playing! — 179
Twenty more feature films and five
TV movies

★

Trivia Time! — 183
Movie trivia gay men should know

★

And the Winner Is! — 184
Five steps to Oscar-party time!

★

Acknowledgments and Answers! — 188

★

Index! — 189

Welcome to *Fabulous!*, a celebratory film book which is based on the notion that there may be a special link between movies and gay people (specifically gay males). But whether you believe this or not, you don't have to be one of "us" (yes, the author is *quite* queer himself) to find something fun *and* familiar within its oh-so beautifully done pages. All people are essentially the same in that we each have something which usually goes much deeper than the simple surface attractions to the cinematic arts. This is what *Fabulous!* is really all about: there being more "here" than meets the eye. However, here are some things to contemplate before jumping inside and taking a look . . .

★

Hollywood makes it a practice of knowing precisely for whom they manufacture their films. (Notice a word is used likening the industry to an assembly line.) Of course, when the business started out, *they* thought everyone was straight, white, middle-class (although these actual terms were not used) adult males and females. Period. Fortunately, as the years advanced, so, too, did the number of audience categories for which movies were produced. Nevertheless, what is created within each genre—specific though those films may be—still cannot satisfy the needs and desires of *every* individual. Speaking plainly, people react personally to pictures. You and I may both be gay (straight, whatever), but this doesn't mean either of us will like a movie just because it is marketed directly to us or for identical reasons, and we probably won't *dislike* it in exactly the same ways, either.

Additionally, while a lot of "reality" can be found in films, whether you can call it actual "truth" is another question entirely. Remember this as *Fabulous!* shifts tones between the subjective and the objective and when terms like "gay" or "queer" (and various derivations thereof) are used to describe films, filmmakers, and stars. Which also does not mean that *Fabulous!* is claiming anyone or anything *is* or *is not* gay. It is necessary to make this statement clear because we still live in a world where associating something—be it person, place, or thing—with "gayness" continues to be taken as somewhat of a negative. (How medieval!) While *Fabulous!* does not feel it is a bad thing to be gay or to have something "gay" about you (in fact, it feels the exact opposite!), it respects that some individuals may not yet have arrived at such an enlightened place. Poor dears.

Furthermore, *Fabulous!* does not wish to be read as an "outing" source, nor does it want to mislead readers into thinking something is what it is not. Actually, true gay orientation (even if it is well documented) is somewhat irrelevant to the cause of *Fabulous!* This book is concerned only with whatever literal and figurative impressions are left behind and whether they can be interpreted as having queer tendencies. To be quite honest, the entire contents of *Fabulous!* are the maybe-fiction, maybe-fact findings of the maybe-just-wishful-thinking writer—and *not* an actual scientific study of its hard-to-substantiate but hard-to-deny subject matter, which could be read by some naysayers as a whole lot of hooey. Hopefully, though, that will not be the conclusion you find upon reaching "the end."

★

But until then, please enjoy the show!

"I vant to be alone."

Above: Spoken famously by moody ballerina Grusinskaya (Greta Garbo) in the archetype movie masterpiece *Grand Hotel* (1932). For more film details, see page 179. *Right: Grand Hotel* scene still, featuring Grusinskaya with the man who would steal her heart (and jewels), Baron Von Geigern (John Barrymore). Everett

Gays and Hollywood. Is there a "reel" connection? Well, *dear readers*, because a book devoted to that very idea is in your hot little hands, the most obvious answer would seem to be "yes." But why not judge for yourself, before taking *Fabulous!*'s word for it? And for some infamous evidence of this relationship, let's go back to the 2000 Academy Awards ceremony . . .

When on that star-spangled night, foxy, silver-haired host Steve Martin remarked that the billion viewers watching the broadcast assumed everyone in the seated audience—luminaries, laypeople, and residents of the entire city of Hollywood alike—were all gay. This was said as a joke, but hadn't the comedian basically just shouted across the globe the belief—*everyone in entertainment is queer!*—which had long been whispered around the world's water coolers? (At this point, it might be prudent to add another bit of *homo*-hearsay: gay men—quite likely those chattering around said drink dispenser, along with a few straight women friends—are the only people actually watching the blessed, blowhard spectacles!)

More proof is certainly available (just ask Liz Taylor for testimony), but is it necessary to make the case? Doubtful. Suffice it to say, Hollywood would still be here today without "us," but it might not have become the town it is—*say what you want about that*—and more than likely the pictures would not have been half as pretty or the actors nearly as glamorous. (The better *queery* might be how strong, not "if" there is a relationship. Is it any stronger than, say, the ties between women, other minorities, and, yet, even heterosexual men and films? I'm afraid no reply should be given, however, as none would satisfy any of the parties involved.)

★

In actuality, *Fabulous!* is not as concerned about establishing the gay connectivity to movies (which is somewhat obvious) as it is interested in exploring how we react to them. The main intention of this book is to show that when it comes to interests and habits, the gay community—because of its historic invisibility—may constitute the most intriguing market catered to by the business.

From the advent of the medium, basically the whole lot of us had to find ourselves where, on the surface, we weren't suppose to be, and, even with the advances wrought by the recent genre of gay film, it still remains today that we *look* at films and *appear* in them differently from any of those other "wonderful people out there in the dark."[1]

Now if that's not intriguing, what is?

★

Skeptical? Of course you are. What would be the fun in agreeing so easily? But honestly, whether you agree isn't as important (yet!) as keeping an open mind for the time being. Starting with exhibits on the following pages, *Fabulous!* will do its damnedest to try and persuade you into seeing things from our side (if you're not already here). And let's revisit this issue at a later time.

Find out the films for all footnoted "quotes" on page 188.

"I'm in no humor tonight to give consequence to the middle classes at play."

Above: Spoken arrogantly by the lofty Mr. Darcy (Laurence Olivier) to Mr. Bingley (Bruce Lester), while being overheard by Elizabeth Bennet (Greer Garson), in *Pride and Prejudice* (1940), the superlative film adaptation of the classic Jane Austen novel. *Left:* Darcy tries in vain to court unmoved Elizabeth. For more details, see page 180. Everett

What is it about movies that attracts people in the first place? They are said to have universal appeal (and *Fabulous!* wholeheartedly agrees with that statement), but is it really possible for *all* types of movies to appeal to *all* types of people? No, not really. While you could be one of those unusual creatures who loves the movies so much that you don't "give a damn" what they're about, most people need some excuse—pure escapism, enlightening messages, a great star, a special director, the genre, among other things—to get them into a theater.

Of course, gay men use the same criteria when making their film selections (hell, we may have invented them!). But, for reasons which form a major part of the basic foundation for *Fabulous!*, they had to twist things around in order to enjoy the very same choices of movies. Why? Because gay men had to change the way they "looked" at films for these two simple, annoying, hurtful, and yet irrefutable causes:

Cause One

For most intents and purposes gays, up until only recently, did not *exist* as far as the general straight population was concerned. Whenever we were acknowledged it was negligible at best, often derogatory, and our behavior was considered highly immoral and essentially illegal.

Cause Two

Up until only recently, for a motion picture to mention or even infer that there could be such a thing as a gay person—SHRIEK!—was also negligible at best, often

derogatory, and our behavior was considered highly immoral and essentially illegal (thanks to a lovely little thing known as the movie code, other industry self-imposed forms of conservative-minded cinema, and innumerable outside censoring groups).

Admittedly, all groups that have been (somewhat dismissively) classified as a minority have their own history of recognition issues with Hollywood, and *Fabulous!* applauds them all for their fortitude, and gains, in the flickering face of daunting odds. By taking just these two causes into account, however, the unique, fragile, and illusive nature of our union, among others in popular culture, should at least be easier to comprehend.

> ★
> ***"Let's not ask for the moon,***
> ***when we have the stars."*** [2]
> ★

Arguably it is the movie's star who determines an individual's ultimate film choice. If he or she is a person's favorite—usually one of many—this actor has the "power" to get them to (using an oft-heard show-biz cliché) "sit through the reading of the phone book." If the star is not, that same person (using another, but more peevish platitude) "couldn't be paid to go and see them." The conventional wisdom then follows that an actor becomes a favorite by their ability (or luck) in choosing roles that consistently find favor among their enamored fans. In fact, never wanting to surprise or stigmatize devotees is the only probable reason why we may never

"A woman is beautiful when she has eight hours' sleep and goes to the beauty parlor every day—and bone structure has a lot to do with it, too."

Above: Spoken by an egocentric Fanny Skeffington (Bette Davis) to her beleaguered husband Job Skeffington (Claude Rains) in the cutting character study *Mr. Skeffington* (1944). *Right:* Fanny is being tended to by her devoted maid Manby (Dorothy Peterson). For more details on this film, see page 180. Everett

see a film in which an actor like, say, Susan Sarandon is playing a homophobe, or, say, Brad Pitt is wearing a dress. *Hmmm.*

After giving yourself time to clear that last "picture" from your head (ewww!), let's use these two actors, whose popularity within the gay community is uncontestable, as examples of what *really* makes an average-Joe player into a "shimmering, glowing star in the cinema firmament."[3] Typically, the most common way to see if they have "it" or not is by determining how the performers in question—remember, we are using Ms. Sarandon and Mr. Pitt as guinea pigs—rate on both of the following two counts:

Do we want to *be like* this person?

- or -

Do we want to *be with* this person?

Not surprisingly, gay men will use this simple "Q&A," too. But because our socio-sexual dynamic in relation to gender is notably reversed so is the outcome:

actress *becomes* role model

-and-

actor *becomes* sex object

This is the hardest part for many straight folk, especially men, to swallow. However, it is an honest report of what actually occurs in the minds of nearly all moviegoing gay males—and something to think about the next time you watch *Thelma and Louise.* But before popping in that DVD, also consider this:

Basic Film Plots: 101

"Boy gets girl" or

"Girl gets boy"

Curiously, too, since gay men's relationship objectives are so similar to those of straight actresses (and much more compatible than with the "PO"—*penis operandi*—of straight actors), many may go an extra step and take a mental leap from their body into that of the female (or male) character. This occurence (hereafter referred to as the *Fabulous! Identification Theory—FIT*, for short) may seem odd to those unaware of its existence, but please remember the following:

FIT *Rule One*

Mentally assimilating is not the same thing as physically putting on lipstick, a bra, and a dress, and going into your place of work (unless, of course, your job happens to be that of a drag queen).

FIT *Rule Two*

Most gay men are no longer aware of doing this themselves, after having done it for so many years—and for now having the option to somewhat openly fantasize sexually about male stars.

FIT *Rule Three*

The act of "identifying" is nothing new to the straight male (or female) moviegoing experience. However, it is usually considered putting oneself into the *action* of the story (because straight men, in particular, supposedly cannot identify with the emotional processes of

"When you speak of this—and you will—be kind."

Above: Spoken by a womanly Laura Reynolds (Deborah Kerr), wife of manly Coach Reynolds (Leif Erickson), as she is about to seduce sensitive boyish Tom Lee (John Kerr) in the "gay" movie milestone *Tea and Sympathy* (1956). *Left:* A shirtless Tom (center) is being torn asunder in an impromptu skirmish by his roommate Al (in white sweatshirt, Darryl Hickman) and fellow college jocks during a school pep rally. For more film details, see page 180. Everett

straight women; while it is not nearly as much of a quandary for gay men).

★

Now that *Fabulous!* has established the bond between gay men and female actresses (it did, didn't it?), let's continue by bringing up that favorite of all films for gay men: the "woman's picture." (If you thought musicals you are not exactly wrong, or right, but they are being saved for individual dissection.)

Gay men have long been fans of *filmes du femmes* and for mainly the same reason(s) we gravitate to actresses: their fight to be seen, heard, and loved as equals in a "heterosexual man's world." Notably, this *gay*-genial genre began showing up around WWII, when men went off to fight and in the wake of departing male thespians female stars picked up their slack in absentia. The results, as anyone who follows the history of movies knows, was a beauteous bounty of distaff-dominant features never before or since equaled in the output of filmdom. This concentration of "classics" from some fifty years ago, however, leaves many with the feeling that they, and their happy fans, are a tad out of touch with serious thinkers and forward thinking. *Fabulous!* is well aware of the strong possibility of appearing editorially sedentary by featuring the usual suspects—Bette, Joan, Judy, and others—along with replays of their plentiful product. But *Fabulous!* moves right past this problem by presenting a variety of the old *and* new, to reflect the (hoped-for) diversity of thought among gay men. Just bear this in mind, no group can have any *real* future without honestly understanding and embracing its past. These lovely ladies (and the far from mellow dramas

they made) helped form the very shape of our present-day "gay" culture. To withhold credit for their contributions would be criminal. *Fabulous!* prefers to come clean about it and let them shine on.

★

Speaking of the "ladies," there are groups into which gay men like to organize their favorites (because we don't want them roaming around at will!), and such groupings pop up in places throughout *Fabulous!* No doubt these listings (and others of different categories) will start heated discussions about whether someone or something should or shouldn't have been included. *Fabulous!* is aware of the possible dissension this may cause, but thought it would be interesting, troublemaking fun to do it anyway. Be on the lookout for them! (Please note that in its attempt to mention as many as possible, *Fabulous!* will name a film only once, even if it is suitable for placement in other categories.)

★

"Now, why would a guy wanna be with another guy? Security?" [4]

★

Despite the reality that many male stars are quite hesitant to accept or even acknowledge us as fans, we still love them. We really do. Nevertheless, while gay men appreciate a good *mano*-logue, constant talk makes the going tough, and we definitely prefer guys' sight *over* sound.

"As far as I'm concerned 'art' is just a guy's name."

Above: Spoken drunkenly by Bob Merrick (Rock Hudson), just as he is about to pass out in the home of Edward Randolph (Otto Kruger), an older male artist, in the film *Magnificent Obsession* (1954). *Right:* At the airport, an accidentally blinded Helen Phillips (in sunglasses, Jane Wyman) is met by her friend and nurse, Nancy Ashford (Agnes Moorehead), center, and stepdaughter, Joyce Phillips (Barbara Rush), also from this Douglas Sirk–directed "weepie." See page 180 for more film details. Everett

More remarkable than the gay man's same-sex attraction—well, duh!—is how this contrasts with his seeming lack of understanding of the mind-set of the straight male actor. However, the gay man's *supposed* absence of this comprehension is balanced by his growing awareness of the large number of actors from whom the modern-day dandy can feel much more acceptance, is often much more physically attracted to, and to whom he has no trouble expressing his affection. But just remember that in today's world what is easily recognizable and openly revealed was, in years past, only so by dint of not much more than an unspoken gesture or two. Speaking of (or writing about) men to whom others are attracted is possible only because gay men before us fought to no longer keep their love a "secret." We should all thank our lucky stars for now having the option to say what we think—out loud. (Or should those "lucky stars" thank us?)

Also, do not count gay men totally clueless or uncaring when it comes to *uber*-straight actors. Actually, gay men are quite like the movies' "good girls" in that we understand these "bad boys" quite well, even though they may bring us harm and heartache. The fact that many readers think otherwise is because some beliefs are just too damned easy to believe. One of those well-known, hard-to-quell rumors is that gay men and straight guys don't mix. (We do, just not openly. Our publicity and marketing people think it would be too confusing.) Another "great lie" would have you believe that all gay men have a corner on the creative and performing arts markets. *Sugarpie*, not all gay men are the "creative types"—and many would rather be watching football, out tinkering under the hood of a car, hooking worms, or some such Neanderthalish nonsense. (Yes, they are out there. Can you believe it?)

★

We should take advantage of this still-musky moment and touch on the topic of "homoeroticism," a very important aspect of movies to discuss because its *indirectness* was (and is) often the gay man's only *direct* link to movies.

Now arguments have been made that many an attractive actor can make even the most "man's man" movie into a poofy pleasure just by virtue of his virile presence (any Vin Diesel movie will serve as a good example of this phenomenon), and even those men on film who are close-mouthed when it comes to anything sounding remotely "queer" about their careers have *all* had their curious "man-baiting" moments. But it takes more than just a handsome hunk or some horny histrionics for a film to be deemed a *he*-roic work of homoeroticism. The real key is in keeping the film's bent "under wraps," which then allows viewers to uncover—*the truth*. To the dismay of filmmakers, often the straighter a film is the gayer it can become. Conversely, real gay content spoils the surprise and will take it out of the queer running. (A few notable homoerotic no-shows, because each features a rather obvious "gay" scene, are *Deliverance*, *Midnight Express*, and *Lawrence of Arabia*.)

Curiously, the gains which the gay community has made over the last few years may have fomented a noticeable loss in the appearance of the *truly* homoerotic film. Nowadays it is assumed that many of our cinematic needs are being tended to by pornography

"Blah, blah, blah."

Above: Spoken dismissively at her former husband's funeral by extremely aged actress Madeline Ashton (Meryl Streep) in the bizarre and bitchy comedy *Death Becomes Her* (1992) to her reluctant longtime friend and enemy, writer Helen Sharp (Goldie Hawn). *Left:* Early on, in a theater dressing room, Mad awaits the arrival of her acquaintance, Hel. For more film details, see page 179. Kobal

and the genre of gay film, neither of which need hide its homosexual content. And current mainstream moviemakers, cognizant of past sexual subterfuge among un- and aware predecessors, are leery if any parts of their movies appear "queer"—with the exception of the ineffectively effete—which may put out also-savvy straight patrons. But readers should not fret. Homo-hidden treasures still appear (for instance, *Spiderman*, 2002), just with eros-exasperating irregularity. While waiting for the next one to appear on the horizon, you can occupy your private moments with a selection listed within the pages of *Fabulous!* Ah, such a tease!

"I'm no longer a queen—I'm a woman."

✮ "Mr. DeMille, I'm ready for my close-up." [5] ✮

While onscreen "homosexiness" may always be an area of contention for Hollywood, its less salacious brother, "Mr. Gay Sensibility," has not run into the same Tinseltown obstacles, thanks in large part to an aesthetic that can easily be made more palatable to the public than erotica—and therefore is not as jeopardizing to all-important revenues in the way that gay sexuality can stop the flow cold. Also, *queer*-ification of pictures could hardly be avoided completely with such large numbers of gays working in the business. Hence, many are stuffed full of gayness, and the person most responsible for stuffing them is usually the director (whom gay men look for after actresses and actors when selecting a film). But as easily as a director can guide his (or her) film in our general vicinity, and *Fabulous!* includes the work of

Above: Spoken exultantly by Cleopatra (Claudette Colbert) to Marc Antony (Henry Wilcoxon), whom she realizes she truly loves, in the 1934 Cecil B. DeMille film version of the oft-told tale of the seductive Egyptian ruler. *Right:* Scene still of *Cleopatra*, featuring Wilcoxon and Colbert being tended to by a soldier and a slave. For more film details, see page 179. Kobal

many whom one would expect, there seem to be fewer recent entrants who can or want to. Ironically, as society has become somewhat more accepting of us as a group, Hollywood is discouraging attracting a "sensible" audience with "style" in favor of casting a wider net of "substance," which usually appears in the form of hundreds of special-effects shots. Again, gay men may have found themselves in a position of two steps forward and one step back: we are gaining recognition but may have lost choices. (Thankfully, *Fabulous!* has plenty to show while we ready to advance again.)

✮ "Because I just went 'gay' all of a sudden!" [6] ✮

Maybe now is as good a time as any to fully address the subject of actual "gay" films and why, to those astute observers who may already have noticed, none are featured in *Fabulous!*

First, just because a film is made for us expressly or has familiar content does not mean it is appreciated by gay men. It would still have to earn its place among so many beloved non-gay choices. Second, being "gay" doesn't necessarily mean it will add anything to the understanding of our experience of film. Third, including gay films might be too literal; the uniqueness of this relationship is better seen figuratively, as when movies anticipated our attendance but did not go out of their way to invite us. Fourth, it would take very little effort to compile a grouping of gay films, and the simplistic structure did not appeal to the masochism of the author

(no pain, no gain!). You will find in *Fabulous!* lots of films that could be classified as "gay friendly" or "positive," and, while they were not deliberately chosen for this reason, a few may be perceived as "anti-gay." Just remember, all of the films here are relative to our position in society at the time of each release. *Fabulous!* would like to add that it fully appreciates the rise of the gay film market, but sees it as a mixed blessing. More often than not, we still find ourselves "invisible" or relegated to secondary roles in mainstream productions, and while there has been a rise in the quantity of gay genre films, the quality of the output so far is contestable. However, there have been clear exceptions that *Fabulous!* wholeheartedly encourages you watch out for, and here are its ten list-toppers:

The Adventures of Priscilla, Queen of the Desert (1996)
Another Country (1984)
The Boys in the Band (1970)
Gods and Monsters (1998)
Longtime Companion (1990)
Maurice (1987)
My Beautiful Laundrette (1985)
Parting Glances (1986)
Victim (1961)
The Wedding Banquet (1993)

Lastly, specifically about the category of general film genres—and which ones attract us—it would be imprudent for readers to believe that just because a person is gay he will like, say, musicals, all "women's pictures," or that grand "daddy" of them all,

the gladiator flick. To assume such, one would also have to say we are all witty wags with buff bodies, right? Nope. Again, only part of the gay population loves the movies. Most are just average, likable guys with only a passing interest. Why, some don't even care about the Oscars or what the stars are wearing! (Quick, the smelling salts!)

Perhaps the reason why people think gay men and, in particular, musicals are so harmoniously intertwined is that these films are pure fantasy (*although all films really are*) and that we seem especially susceptible to the "fantastic" because it provides solace from life's sometimes unaccepting reality. But is this true love in all cases, even of truly bad musicals? No way. There is also constant chatter about gay men and "camp" films (many of which you will see in *Fabulous!*). Assuredly, we appreciate what it represents: hilarious humiliation mixed with high expectations. But again, usually only those who care the most for filmdom's finest *and* lowest can chuckle knowingly at what is being utterly undermined. Without this background the pictures often appear innocuous, inept, not always funny, and hardly "gay."

However, all gay filmgoers do share an affection or at least a consistent attentiveness to one genre-ish type of movie: those that deal with the experience of "acceptance" (along with the adjuncts of "coming out" and "fitting in"). On some level, every one of us had to go through this step, and often alone. Watching it play out in a movie, we see that all people participate in this process. Knowing that gays and straights have this as common ground is a good place to end one chapter and begin another that shows by example . . .

"Henry! There's somebody coming up the stairs!"

Above: Spoken desperately by a bedridden Leona Stevenson (Barbara Stanwyck) to her husband, Henry Stevenson (Burt Lancaster), on the phone, in the suspense thriller film version of the hit radio broadcast *Sorry, Wrong Number* (1948). *Left:* Mrs. Stevenson primps in her bed. For more film details, see page 180. Kobal

Now Showing!

"When you throw a lamb chop into a hot oven, what's gonna keep it from gettin' done?"

Leftt: Mrs. Howard Fowler (Rosalind Russell) tries to get Crystal Allen (Joan Crawford) to "come clean" in a scene from *The Women* (1939). Everett. *Above:* Spoken by cosmetics salesgirl Crystal to cosmetics counter maid Lulu (Butterfly McQueen) in an attempt to have her prepare a meal for the former's date with a married man, also from *The Women*. For more film details, see page 175. *Right:* Rex Stetson (Rock Hudson) easily carries off inebriated Tony Walters (Nick Adams), the would-be courtier of decorator Jan Morrow (Doris Day), in a scene from the "bedroom" comedy *Pillow Talk* (1959). For more film details, see page 128. Everett

This section is the core of *Fabulous!* Its gathering of films representing the best (and yes, possibly the worst) that moviemakers have to offer illuminates the book's preceding and pending arguments. But their presence will no doubt cause many debates, too. *Really, a group of seventy-five film favorites, as presented by one hyper-opinionated sissy!? Holy hissy-fits, how audacious!* But before taking *Fabulous!* and its author to task for the affrontery, please consider that the offerings are not an official gathering. *They are suggestions.* (Could they be otherwise, knowing how damned hard it is to get us to agree on anything?) To those still not swayed, there is good reason why each film is included. Whether it is a scene, the dialogue, a star, or some other *queer*-ish aspect—from the subtle to the "slap in the face"—every selection has something to say for, about, or even against the triumphs, trials, and sometimes questionable taste levels of gay men and our culture.

★

No doubt, there are those who may continue to wonder how it is that *Fabulous!* and its author could know which movies to feature. Well, here's the best explanation: the great "gayvine." This communication system goes into motion when one gay man tells of a "discovery" to another. Then, from man to man, details quickly criss-cross the community, leaving behind critical information as to the persons, places, and things we should all be on the lookout for. Since movies are a particularly favorite form of recommendation, it is rare to find one of us who doesn't know at least by name the choices filling our library of essential films. (Note: He may not have seen them all, but he knows their names.)

In addition, you will see that a notable amount of well-regarded films are not represented. Among those missing are *Gone With the Wind, Casablanca*, and *Citizen Kane*. There is good reason why these are not "Now Showing," too. All of the films in this book were selected because they complemented the editorial by dealing specifically with the gay experience of moviegoing. Even though many mainstream (that is, straight) films are well liked by gay men, to include those listed above would just muddy up the works. Further—*and this is* trés *important*—their absence does not mean that we tend to overlook films which could be classified as "straight." We most definitely find many of them enjoyable to watch (which should be evident by the fact that the majority of the films in *Fabulous!* are actually classified as "mainstream"). Additionally, many of these so-called classic films are *always* celebrated, and now it's our turn to have a party. *Fabulous!* does apologize, though, to those whose "gay" choices did not make the cut (which includes many of the author's own). Maybe next time.

Warning! Warning! Warning!

Fabulous! is written mainly using the questionably valid precepts of what is considered *stereotypic* gay male behavior. No doubt this will offend some readers. For what it's worth, the author acknowledges that the book's contents do not speak for the entire community. However, he can assure readers that if they watch all seventy-five films they will come away feeling a little "gayer" than when they started. You have been warned.

And now, without further delay . . .

"You want some advice? Well, here's some advice from me to you: lay off the caramels."

Above: Spoken snidely by inmate Roxie Hart (Renee Zellweger) in retaliation to Velma Kelly (Catherine Zeta-Jones) in the landmark musical *Chicago* (2002). *Left:* Velma prepares to perform "I Can't Do It Alone" for Roxie. For more film details see page 67. Kobal

1949. MGM. Directed by George Cukor. Starring Spencer Tracy, Katharine Hepburn, David Wayne, Tom Ewell, Judy Holliday, and Jean Hagen.

★

The basic story: Two lawyers, married to each other, find themselves working on different sides of the same high-profile court case. The wife is the defender of a woman accused of attempting to murder her husband—and her spouse is the prosecutor.

★

Tracy and Hepburn are a perfect *FIT* for gay moviegoers. Though there was never any doubt he was a "man's man," Spence always seemed more the wise pater than the brutish male type. And Kate, while every inch a woman, was hardly willing to suppress (any more than absolutely necessary) her Yankee independence in deference to filmdom's preferred portraits of women as the "weaker sex." Coupled with their natural physical chemistry, the two created an impression of equality unlike the usual unequal male-female screen couplings, and thus made it quite easy for us to see ourselves in his laceups and her pumps.

Out of nine movies they made together, *Rib* was definitely their most sophisticated in terms of a modern story line. Throughout the film, Tracy (Adam Bonner) argues that his legal eaglette wife (Amanda Bonner) bends the law, which is underscored by the period's new debate over the roles of the sexes in postwar society. But more "gay" noteworthy, while Tracy's alpha maleness is often tempered by Hepburn's feminine wiles—in this "guy vs gal" comedy—the more telling sexual set-tos occur via threeways with their nelly neighbor across the hall, Kip Lurie.

(How fey is that name?) However, as a Cole Porterish composer (played by David Wayne), whose queenly behavior is obviously meant to elevate Tracy to king of his domain, Kip is the one smudge on an otherwise spotless supporting cast of characters—which includes Judy Holliday's pre–*Born Yesterday* turn as the reluctant guntoter and Jean Hagen as the "other woman."

Granted, there is still something notable about Kip's presence (who, thanks to Wayne, bears a resemblance to Jack in TV's *Will & Grace* in looks and mannerisms). While not an especially flattering portrayal, it shows awareness on the part of director Cukor (and writers Ruth Gordon and Garson Kanin, AAN) that in their chic city setting our kind would have "played a part." (Note: Kip's sexuality is mainly inferred, and referred to only once by way of a snide remark from Tracy in reply to the quote on the left.)

★

Adam's *"gay" ribs:*
- Hope Emerson, as Olympia LaPere, the dykiest performing act this side of the circus's bearded lady.
- The jury being asked to imagine plaintiff Ewell (Warren Attinger) as a woman, and defendant Holliday (Doris Attinger) as a man.
- Hepburn as the definite dish in her off-the-shoulder black evening gown. What a stunner!

Adam's *companion:*
Desk Set (1957) is decidedly the team's foofiest, with researcher Kate tightly cinched in *beaucoup* high-necked shirtwaists and Spence in mismatched socks.

"You've got me so convinced, I may even go out and become a woman."

Above: Spoken lovingly by Kip Lurie (David Wayne) to Amanda Bonner (Katharine Hepburn) to goad her husband. *Right:* Husband Adam Bonner (Spencer Tracy), Kip, and Amanda in the couple's kitchen. Everett

1970. Universal (AAN). Directed by George Seaton. Starring Burt Lancaster, Dean Martin, Jean Seberg, Helen Hayes (AA), Van Heflin, Jacqueline Bisset, George Kennedy, and Maureen Stapleton (AAN).

★

The basic story: A major city airport, and its manager, are besieged with the biggest snowstorm in years, a stuck plane creating an unusable runway, redirected noisy flights making neighboring residents quite testy, and an airborne jet full of passengers and crew with their own set of problems caused by an exploded bomb and the hole it left in the fuselage.

★

Most people outside of the "group" don't know this, so *Fabulous!* will let you in on a little gay secret: we are crazy for the chic world of aviation. But considering that most everyone *assumes* that gay men are either designer-luggage-toting resort-hoppers or slim, salad-serving attendants, how can this affair really be a surprise? Ah, that's because you don't know the real reasons for our "flight" connection, do you? Well, it only has everything to do with jet-setting (which still connotes superclass status, but just in first!) and jets (because of their obvious phallic symbolism). Honestly, you didn't think we were in love with aviation because we actually wanted to fly the planes, did you? Heavens, no!

Now that our aviation attraction has been properly exposed, you should be able to glean why it is that such a jumbo-sized movie as *Airport*—which fully combines flying *and* fabulousness—has landed on the pages of this book. Actually, *Airport* may be too packed with gay goodies. But jamming the aisles—in this case with stars

and strife—allows *Airport* to be classified into two more gay-favorite film areas: one, the "grand hotel" category (to those unfamiliar with the Oscar-winning 1932 original that inspired the name, this type of motion picture revolves around a large cast sharing a central location—herein, for you trivia-minded, the old main terminal in Minneapolis–St. Paul—and intertwining dramatic personal relationships); and two, as a "disaster" flick, because so much of the action occurs on board that damaged plane in the sky, which truthfully makes *Airport* into more of a guilty gay film pleasure, being that we don't tend toward cinematic calamity unless the chaos is as chicly and cleverly confined as it is here.

★

The "gayest" on board Airport:
• John Findlater, as the timid, towheaded Trans Global Airline's concierge Peter Coakley, who escorts the irascible, endearing stowaway Helen Hayes (Mrs. Quonset).
• Sexy stewardess Gwen Meighan (Jackie Bisset) and her cupboard stash of baby-sized booze bottles (nope, don't know any gay attendant who has those around).

Sharing the Airport *terminal:*
• For "jet-set" fans: *Come Fly with Me* (1962). A camp masterpiece with the hunkiest pilot you'll ever want landing on your runway, Hugh O'Brian.
• For "grand hotel" fans: *Hotel* (1966), with humpy Rod Taylor and regal Merle Oberon.
• For "disaster" fans: *The Poseidon Adventure* (1972). Another camp classic, thanks to Carol Lynley's impressive rendering of "The Morning After" and Shelley Winters's impressive rendering of an underwater sea mammal.

"They don't call 'em emergencies anymore, they call 'em Patroni's."

Above: Spoken boisterously by Joe Patroni (George Kennedy) to his wife, Marie Patroni (Jodean Russo), after being asked to help beleaguered airport manager Mel Bakersfield (Burt Lancaster) move a grounded plane. *Left:* On board the soon-to-be exploded 707 are Captain Vernon Demarast (Dean Martin), center, flanked behind on the right by stewardess Gwen Meighan (Jacqueline Bisset). Kobal

All About Eve

1950. Twentieth Century-Fox (AA). Directed by Joseph Mankiewicz (AA). Starring Bette Davis (AAN), Anne Baxter (AAN), George Sanders (AA), Celeste Holm (AAN), Thelma Ritter (AAN), Hugh Marlowe, Gary Merrill, Gregory Ratoff, and Marilyn Monroe.

★

The basic story: A mature stage actress and her best friend, a playwright's wife, take under their wings a seemingly benign young woman. However, their petite protégée has acting aspirations of her own, and the poisonous way she plies her ambitious agenda soon wreaks havoc among all.

★

If one movie were to top the list of nearly every gay man's favorite films, or at the very least a roster representing things integral to a better understanding of gay culture (wow! this sounds important), without a doubt, *Eve* would be that movie. (The only other viable contender is *The Wizard of Oz.*) This is something most would agree upon, even outside the gay community. But if an explanation is necessary as to why this is so, fortunately there are just two fundamental reasons why this film, from among so many to choose, has held up and held its place in our hearts, and they are:

"One About Eve"

Like all movies with the greatest of gay appeal (keeping in mind that *Eve* has a large straight following, too), it is easy to find familiarity among the film's cast members. To test this, just sit a moment and review the entire ensemble. We here at *Fabulous!* will wait. (Warning: The results of this simple, yet possibly unsettling exami-

nation can undermine the sexual security of your whole world, especially if you're heterosexual. Please proceed with caution.) Are you done? See how there's isn't a single redressed player—especially that "fishwife" Addison DeWitt (George Sanders)—who doesn't fit right in or out of the closet?

"Two About Eve"

Even in its heterosexual context (yeah right, the theater world "straight"!), the film has everything a gay man would want in a movie and wish for in life: the ability to trade timely and witty barbs; lunches at Twenty-One; a triplex in the city; fab clothes; parties with pianists; friends with a country house; meetings with Zanuck; and that your next play should be named *Footsteps on the Ceiling.* The only things not in *Eve* are bona fide hunks, although Marlowe and Merrill are cute and will do in a pinch, and "bloodhounds snapping at your rear."

★

There's something "queer" about Eve:
It's mostly imperceptible, but there is a lesbian edge to the character of Eve Harrington. Look for it with her "arm-in-arm" staircase climb with a fellow female boarder; the tension between her and Bertie (Thelma Ritter); and her cocktail ease in letting Phoebe (Barbara Bates) stay overnight.

Eve's companion:
Mankiewicz's loquacious *A Letter to Three Wives* (1949), starring lovely Linda Darnell, affable Ann Sothern, and jubilant Jeanne Crain.

"Dear Margo, you were an unforgettable Peter Pan. You must play it again some time."

Above: Spoken cattily by Addison DeWitt (George Sanders) to Margo Channing (Bette Davis) upon the latter's expressing dismay that he has shown up at her party for returning lover Bill Sampson (Gary Merrill). *Right:* From left, Eve Harrington (Anne Baxter), Margo, Miss Caswell (Marilyn Monroe), and Addison on the night of Margo's (and gay movie fandom's most infamous) get-together. Kobal

1958. Warner Bros. (AAN). Directed by Morton DaCosta. Starring Rosalind Russell (AAN), Forrest Tucker, Coral Browne, Fred Clark, Roger Smith, Patric Knowles, and Peggy Cass (AAN).

★

The basic story: A Chicago industrialist unexpectedly dies, and his son is sent to live with the man's sister in New York. She turns out to be an extravagent, "madcap" socialite, but one who quickly wins the heart of her young charge. However, she must fight the forces of conventionality to keep him as he grows into adulthood.

★

This is the story of a loving, gregarious, and accepting woman—with a "to-die-for" apartment and wardrobe—who feeds you *cah*-viar the first night you meet, is friendly with lesbians (look fast in that opening party scene!), sends you to a school where they sit around naked eating yogurt, encourages you to mix cocktails years before you can drive, writes scathingly racy autobiographies—and does at-home beauty makeovers! Honestly, what child wouldn't love to live in little Patrick Dennis's world? (Hell, what adult, gay or straight, wouldn't?)

However, the real attraction to *Mame* lies far beyond the promise of living large and lavishly twenty-four hours a day, seven days a week. Frankly, few movies—or movie heroines—have ever thrown their "arms" around the people and pleasures of the world with such obvious fondness and fervor. But what may be most remarkable, *little lambs*, is that this film was made during the arch-conservative fifties (though notably, toward the decade's end), and while its embracing tone tickled many it troubled quite a few, too. A telling parallel can be drawn with some mainstream critics at the time who felt Roz Russell's powerhouse performance and the film was too-*too*—the b-a-s-t-a-r-d-s! But audiences flocked to the banquet and ate it up anyway, from the bedazzling credits to the final staircase climb. So there!

★

Mame's "queerest" relations:

• The true story of author Patrick Dennis (aka Edward Everett Tanner III) may be as interesting as *Mame* is entertaining: he was a married father, but at the very, *very* least bisexual; he wrote many bestselling books, including this two-million seller, the fantabulous *Little Me* (a gay-lit essential), yet worked as a butler for—get ready, 'cuz this'll really french your fries—Mr. Ray Kroc of McDonald's fame(!), before dying nearly penniless.

• Hunky actor Roger Smith, who played "older" Patrick, went on to marry and manage the career of none other than Miss Ann-Margret.

• Impossibly chic Coral Browne (Vera Charles)—also longtime wife of handsome horrormeister Vincent Price—would go on to suckle at the breast of Sue Lyon in the lesbo-cult classic *The Killing of Sister George.*

• Costume designer Orry-Kelly's exquisite ensembles.

Auntie's *companion:*
Watch *Mame,* the disastrous 1974 film version of the hit Broadway musical version of the book (and film) starring a too-aged Lucille Ball in the title role. But only, though this is reason enough, to see co-star Beatrice Arthur (Vera Charles) re-create the role that won her a Tony—and our early gay esteem.

"I never had a child. But after all, I'm an actress, I can imagine."

Above: Spoken justifyingly by Vera Charles (Coral Browne) to Mame Dennis (Rosalind Russell) upon learning that the latter may be losing custody of her nephew. *Left:* Publicity still of Rosalind Russell as Mame Dennis. Kobal

Babe

36

1995. Universal (AAN). Directed by Chris Noonan (AAN). Starring James Cromwell (AAN), Magda Szubanski, Christine Cavanaugh (the voice of Babe the pig), Miriam Margolyes (the voice of Fly the female sheepdog), Danny Mann (the voice of Ferdinand the duck), and Hugo Weaving (the voice of Rex the male sheepdog).

★

The basic story: A little piglet won as a prize at a local fair believes he can become anything he wants. With the help of the farm animals at his new home, the intuitive farmer, the sheepdogs, and the sheep, he desires to be a sheepherder, and eventually succeeds.

★

Everybody say "awww." Now, if you are not familiar with this sugary-sweet sound, or its correct time and usage, perhaps you are past due taking a day trip with a gay friend to his favorite knickknack, curio, or card shop, where an example of its proper pitch and placement will be quickly forthcoming. To those still unfamiliar, this gay utterance is the "so cute" equivalent to that which is vocalized by straight females at the sight of newborn babies and needlepointed pillows. Since *Babe* is a movie about *awww*-dorable animals—and specifically a sensitive squealer who triumphs over insurmountable odds—it has this *awww*-some power to render gay men helpless to stop themselves from purchasing tickets. (Note: The sound will likely come just by viewing the *awww*-companying photograph.)

However, there is the issue of *Babe* being included in *Fabulous!* just because it is a "kiddie" picture, and, in tandem, the belief that gay men do not like children—

and children's things. But *Fabulous!* begs to differ, and offers these three reasons why:

Childish Excuse #1

Honestly, one has to wonder where these rumors start! Gay men love the li'l darlins, dearly. (Just don't expect us to change diapers, babysit, or be happy seated near one on an airplane.)

Childish Excuse #2

Being "for children" hardly means a film can't entertain adults. The best, like most of Chuck Jones's Bugs Bunny film shorts, appeal to both children (with lots of bright colors) *and* their ticket-buying, maturer chaperones (with witty story lines).

Childish Excuse #3

What pet-owning gay man hasn't wished that his furry or feathered friend could say a few words, especially of consolation, like "That guy was a jerk" or "You can do better"? In fact, the Oscar-winning "talking" animal angle is the most compelling reason of all to watch.

This little piggy had his fair share, but isn't the only kid flick to have gay market appeal. Here are five which have had us squealing in our pens:

★

Chicken Run (2000)
The 5,000 Fingers of Doctor T (1953)
Ice Age (2002)
The Muppet Movie (1979)
Willy Wonka and the Chocolate Factory (1971)

"That'll do pig, that'll do."

Above: Spoken fondly by Farmer Hoggett (James Cromwell) to Babe (voice of Christine Cavanaugh) after the little piglet performs a successful act of sheepherding. *Right:* Publicity shot of Babe. Kobal

The Bad and the Beautiful

1952. MGM. Directed by Vincente Minnelli. Starring Kirk Douglas (AAN), Lana Turner, Walter Pidgeon, Dick Powell, Barry Sullivan, Gloria Grahame (AA), Gilbert Roland, Leo G. Carroll, Paul Stewart, and Elaine Stewart.

★

The basic story: The bad and beautiful tale of a producer who went from B pictures to the top of the Hollywood pack and back down again is told in flashbacks by onetime friends and collaborators—a studio executive, a skilled director, a noted writer, and a lovely actress—as they consider working again with the man who used them to succeed.

★

By finding ourselves in the unenviable but often necessary position of "playacting" for our own protection, gay men know well the strong though culpable need for making false appearances. So naturally when the land of make-believe removes its own famed façade, albeit temporarily, it is cause for us to celebrate. This is also quite remarkable, in that gay men seem to find such pleasure in tearing down many of the things in Tinseltown they helped to put up.

Perhaps no one knew this perfidiousness or how to attractively parlay it better than director Vincente Minnelli, who, by the time of *Bad*'s release, was already a favorite of gay moviegoers. Of course, this adoration was not spoken publicly, nor was it possible for a man standing on the threshold of Hollywood's closet to return the thanks to such a private audience. Nonetheless, because of his "stylish" handling of many an MGM magical musical (*An American in Paris*, 1951), light comedy (*Father of the Bride*, 1950), and period drama (*Madame Bovary*, 1949), the "sensibilities" of the man making it happen were obvious, as was why the studio entrusted him with this particular "behind-the-scenes" project—knowing who, among others, would end up watching.

The finished film was quite something to behold—and an exquisite example of the kind of film many would say the industry doesn't (and can't) make anymore. But still, in the grand Hollywood tradition of lily-gilding, some of *Bad* may be *too* beautiful. This might have been the result of having a director with such a "theatrical" background. However, for a section of the general population known for choosing style over substance, it's a scene-for-scene-stealing treat. Bon appetit!

★

The "baddest" in Beautiful*:*
• A *slinky* Elaine Stewart slithering down Douglas's staircase. Could she be what toymakers had in mind?

The "gayest" in Bad*:*
• Gloria Grahame as Rosemary Bartlow, the Dixie queen desperate to be dethroned.

Along with Minnelli, here are five more directors, and a film for each, whose output has proved time and again soothing to the "sensitive" eye:

★

Anthony Asquith's *The Importance of Being Earnest* (1952)
Henry Koster's *Flower Drum Song* (1961)
Ernst Lubitsch's *Ninotchka* (1939)
George Sidney's *Viva Las Vegas* (1964)
Charles Walters's *Lili* (1953)

"James Lee, you have a very naughty mind—I'm happy to say."

Above: Spoken naughtily by Rosemary Bartlow (Gloria Grahame) to her writer husband, James Lee Bartlow (Dick Powell). *Left:* Georgia Lorrison (Lana Turner), center, flanked on the left by Syd Murphy (Paul Stewart), standing by Henry Whitfield (Leo G. Carroll), on the right by Victor "Gaucho" Ribera (Gilbert Roland), and also standing Harry Pebbel (Walter Pidgeon). Everett

The Bad Seed

1956. Warner Bros. Directed by Mervyn LeRoy. Starring Nancy Kelly (AAN), Patty McCormack (AAN), Henry Jones, Eileen Heckart (AAN), Evelyn Varden, William Hopper, Paul Fix, Jesse White, and Gage Clarke.

★

The basic story: The perfect house, wife, husband, and daughter. All is well until things begin unraveling after a medal-winning classmate is found drowned at a school outing and suspicion is cast on the too-sweet young girl who desperately wanted the award herself.

★

Could there be a direct correlation between wearing pigtails and being helplessly and hopelessly driven to commit murder? Quite possibly. Do the chances increase if you add a red-and-white dotted Swiss dress and patent leather shoes (with, let us not forget, metal taps)? Was this just, mercifully, a "fifties thing," or do twenty-first-century girls still have to endure this kind of unstylish assault to the senses? Hopefully not. But the old-fashioned finery of the murdering moppet at the center of this film was not the joke of some child-hating costumer (Moss Mabry) determined to make his *Seed* look bad. No, not at all. The intention was just the obvious opposite: to make her look as much like the beloved "good girl" as was possible, before uncovering the unlovable news underneath: that she has quite the dark side and may just be killing off kindly upstairs neighbors, cowering class rivals, and cuckoo caretakers.

But wait, the exaggeration doesn't stop with the film's juvenile ensembles. What may be even more "in your face" than the girlish getups—and mother's mas-terfully applied maquillage and menacing manicure—are the bellicose performances produced by every actor present, which seemed directed by LeRoy to play to a theater's back row. (*Hello! Can you hear me out there?*) This bellowing brings to mind the story's successful stage origins, but it obviously did not offend the eyes and ears of moviegoers, as the film, too, became a hit. (Note: For trivialists and award followers, Kelly, McCormack, Heckart, Varden, and Jones all re-created their original stage roles, and Kelly won the 1955 Tony Award for Best Actress in a Play.)

High-pitched hysterics aside, you may wonder what makes this midnight movie especially "gay." Well, *Fabulous!* feels that its classic campiness *queerly* qualifies it, but that may not be enough to persuade more persnickety readers. Here then is another thought: is pernicious and pretentious Rhoda Penmark, who murdered for jewelry and over the return of her adored and useful tap shoes, so like many gay boys who behave(d) just as brattishly and above it all, that perchance we recognize a bit of ourselves? But for the record, wouldn't Claude Daigle, the poor unseen dear offed for his penmanship medal—*ahem!*—be the odds-on grow-up-to-be-gay favorite?

A very Bad *companion:*
Village of the Damned (1960) features George Sanders as the schoolteacher in a tiny English town terrorized by bleached-blond boys and girls from outer space. Quick, look away!

"Daddy, how long do lovebirds live?"

Above: Spoken too inquisitively by Rhoda Penmark (Patty McCormack) to her adoring father (William Hopper) after learning that she will inherit the birds of her upstairs neighbor, but only after the aged woman's death. *Right:* Christine Penmark (Nancy Kelly) confronting her daughter, Rhoda, about all the awful things that have been happening recently. Kobal

1988. Mainline (Germany). Directed by Percy Adlon. Starring Marianne Sägebrecht, Jack Palance, C.C.H. Pounder, Christine Kaufmann, Monica Calhoun, and Darron Flagg.

★

The basic story: A traveler separated from her husband seeks refuge in a roadside establishment run by an owner with quite a few problems of her own. After initial difficulties, the women become friends and try to make the best of their bleak surroundings.

★

Imagine a movie that stars one really "big" babe (Sägebrecht) with a penchant for neatening things and a "prisonly" proprietress (Pounder) who can't keep anything in order. (If this already sounds to you a little like *The Odd Couple* gender-updated, you get some *Fabulous!* bonus points.) Add a mystical touch here, a few dirty edges there, and you have a movie the boys cannot resist.

Ah, but the real gay attraction of this artsy movie lies within its message of "acceptance." Frequently a part of many favorites, as noted in the Introduction, this theme of inclusion is often needed to gain our seal of approval, and in *Café* is appetizingly served two ways:

The "Relationship"

Things do get off to a muddled start between the two women. Pounder convinces herself that newly arrived Sägebrecht is a "perv" (what with all those *queer* clothes) and doesn't appreciate having her office uncluttered via this "cleaning machine" from out of nowhere, mainly because it just stirs up trouble in her own messy mind. But they do come together in time for the curtain to go up. *A-one and a-two . . .*

Yep, it's showtime, and through some unexplained, magical happenings, the duo fall into an impromptu routine—with plenty of sand handy for the ol' soft shoe—which becomes a major desert attraction. However, a rift reappears when the now-joyful café owner feels vulnerable to the entertaining new experience. In defense, she bids her odd partner adieu. But with "Mrs. Clean" gone the pixie dust also vanishes, and the innkeeper finds herself missing both. The gay moral of the story: accept a person for who they are, not for whom you want them to be, and it will bring to both of your lives much singing and dancing.

The "Song"

The second way *Café* imparts its message of acceptance is more subtle but just as memorable. By sending out a clear signal of love and longing, the Oscar-nominated "Calling You" does what all great movie songs do: plants a haunting and hypnotic refrain in your brain that runs on replay well after the film is finished.

Suckers for the "soft sell" of a song, gay men keep the memory of many in their songbook of favorites. Here is a *homo*-nious group of five:

★

"I Wish I Didn't Love You So" (*Perils of Pauline*, 1947)

"Last Dance" (*Thank God It's Friday*, 1978)

"Secret Love" (*Calamity Jane*, 1953)

"When She Loved Me" (*Toy Story 2*, 1999)

"You'll Never Know" (*Hello Frisco, Hello*, 1943)

"She ain't got nothin' but a suitcase filled with men's clothing!"

Above: Spoken by distraught innkeeper Brenda (C.C.H. Pounder) to Sheriff Arnie (Apesanahkwat). *Left:* Brenda and Jasmin (Marianne Sägebrecht) at the conclusion of their "act." Everett

Barefoot in the Park

1967. Paramount. Directed by Gene Saks. Starring Robert Redford, Jane Fonda, Charles Boyer, Mildred Natwick (AAN), Herb Adelman, Mabel Albertson, and Fritz Feld.

★

The basic story: Two newlyweds move into a very small, sixth-story walk-up apartment in Greenwich Village and find that they may not have as much in common as they thought. Tensions grow, things are said, but eventually saner heads prevail.

★

Really, how cute were "carefree" Jane Fonda and "conservative" Robert Redford in their younger days? Didn't they just make a darling—and oh-so-"gay"—couple? Here is where *Fabulous!* might be crossing the line, so to speak, as their mixed-and-matched pairing is admittedly similar to nearly every young couple, gay or straight. But still, it is startling to see how much alike we all are, isn't it? And what about that adorable skylit flat with the funky neighbors and the sexually indeterminate couple downstairs? Now that's "gay," right? And isn't that just *so* New York City, a top queer locale, to live like such bohemians? And by setting things in the inner-city jungle (to a spiffy Neal Hefti score), Corie and Paul do instantly appear a touch gayer than if the pair lived out in the burbs, don't they? Well, *Fabulous!* thinks so.

But maybe the gayest touch in *Park* comes not in the action or setting. With *Barefoot*, playwright/screenwriter Neil Simon was at the beginning of a long winning streak and his weapons of choice were his words, most of them very witty ones (and you know how much we love clever conversation). So is it with dishy dialogue that *Barefoot* wins our hearts? Unfortunately not yet, because herein lies a prose problem. What Simon wrote well sometimes did not read well onscreen. Sometimes. In order for the lines to be successful without the immediate guffaw of a goosed live audience they needed to be delivered by just the right people. Fortunately, in *Barefoot* Simon was blessed with many and, in particular, one of acting's best messengers: Mildred Natwick, a shining member of that near-vanished breed, the character actress, who was able to enliven every scene in which she appeared. So now you have the "gayest" reason of all to take a walk in this *Park*.

★

A Barefoot *companion film:*
Apartment for Peggy (1948). Jeanne Crain and William Holden star as newlyweds who rent an attic from Edmund Gwenn, in a film as sweet as spun sugar.

Sadly, Mildred Natwick and many of her peers have all but disappeared from the big and small screen (this Emmy-winning Snoop Sister passed away in 1994). But gay men are still "mad about the gals," going so far as to watch the unwatchable if one of their faves is playing (we are nothing, if not devoted). Here are five more funny ladies (and a film) whom we are always falling for:

★

Eileen Brennan in *Private Benjamin* (1980, AAN)
Joan Cusack in *Working Girl* (1988, AAN)
Jean Hagen in *Singin' in the Rain* (1952, AAN)
Marjorie Main in *The Egg and I* (1947, AAN)
Margaret Rutherford in *The VIPs* (1963, AA)

"I feel like we've died and gone to heaven—only we had to climb up."

Above: Spoken breathlessly by Mrs. Ethel Banks (Mildred Natwick) to her son-in-law Paul Bratter (Robert Redford). *Right:* Commencing their honeymoon carriage ride at the Plaza Hotel are newlyweds Paul and Corie Bratter (Jane Fonda). Everett

1959. Twentieth Century-Fox. Directed by Jean Negulesco. Starring Hope Lange, Stephen Boyd, Joan Crawford, Louis Jourdan, Suzy Parker, Martha Hyer, Diane Baker, Brian Aherne, and Robert Evans.

★

The basic story: A trio of "career girls" work for the same publishing company, share the same Manhattan apartment, and experience the same ups and downs with men.

★

From the moment the dreamy Sammy Cahn and Alfred Newman–penned, Johnny Mathis–sung, and Academy Award–nominated theme song floats across the airwaves, viewers have booked passage on a *bon-bon* voyage, with stops in Ports Happiness and Heartache, under the command of three pretty misses. Admirably, these damsels at sea steer their virtuous vessel clear of too many "on the rocks" cocktails, deep-running emotions, and mighty tense waters, but have occasion to run aground at the hands of some horrible harassers. However, they sail most worthily through this sardine-packed assortment of sharkskin-suited swains and fishy-smelling suitors while searching for safe harbor in the arms of just the "right man."

Furthermore, while *Best* can be a tank full of loathsome lotharios ready to spawn at the drop of a fly, now and then it does offer a real catch (Stephen Boyd) when a line is cast correctly. And as for cruising fans, its entire attractive crew of both female and male shipmates is plenty of bait to hook most of us for a few laps around the island of Manhattan. So gentlemen, jump right in, the water's fine!

The "best" of Everything:

• Sensational Suzy Parker, a real-life model-cum-actress "off her nut" in a mind-blowing mise-en-sideways-scène. Don't even think of missing it!

• Heavenly Hope Lange may be too ingenue to be promoted to editor on the strength of weak critiques like "Could be bestseller!," but what a cutie she was!

The "worst" of Everything:

• Repulsive Robert Evans, as the ne'er-do-well who "knocks up" dewy Diane Baker, became a top Hollywood producer (*Chinatown*). Hiss!

• Jaded Joan Crawford, well past her kitten years, as the testiest tigress one could imagine as any woman's boss or any man's mistress. Grrrr!

The "strangest" of Everything:

• Funky fifties period details like coffee in a jar (with deposit!), interoffice smoking, and the acceptability of fanny-pinching male executives!

• Snipped scenes between stately Martha Hyer and her adulterous partner, the studly Donald Harron.

Fans of this film may experience a little "*gay*-jà vu" when watching the cable series *Sex and the City*, reruns of network TV's *The Golden Girls*, and even films like *The Group* (1966) and *Valley of the Dolls* (see page 164). Well, boys and girls, comparisons have been drawn between them all since day one. Even though *Best* may not be the best example of sisterly sorority—and may not be the most enlightening or intelligent—it was there first.

"Now you and your rabbit-faced wife can both go to hell!"

Above: Spoken dejectedly by Amanda Farrow (Joan Crawford) on the telephone to her married lover. *Left:* Scene still of *Best*'s three roomies, from left, Caroline Bender (Hope Lange), Gregg Adams (Suzy Parker), and April Morrison (Diane Baker) toasting at home in their tiny, one-bedroom Manhattan apartment. Kobal

Billy Elliot

2000. Universal (British). Directed by Stephen Daldry (AAN). Starring Jamie Bell, Jean Haywood, Jamie Draven, Gary Lewis, Stuart Wells, Mike Elliot, Billy Fane, Nicola Blackwell, and Julie Walters (AAN).

★

The basic story: A young, motherless boy growing up in a middle-class English mining town is more interested in ballet than he is in the usual masculine pursuits, to the dismay of his out-of-work father.

★

Much is always said and written about the relationships between gay men and their either doting or overbearing mothers. Unfortunately, this leaves less room for notes about interactions with our fathers. This gay cultural dominance of the "mother-son" dynamic coupled with a typical preference for "softer" cinematic choices (female-ish film) results in an overwhelming amount of seemingly emasculated movies among the *Fabulous!* list. However, *Billy* is given a spot because "he" is one of those rare sensitive film types who clearly moves us, but whose story is not *so* queer as to stop the real "menfolk" from appearing alongside.

And being that it is predominantly male-oriented, *Billy* initially can be viewed as a "man's" movie. It does become rather quickly apparent, though, that this story of men comes from a decidedly gay perspective. The reason why *Fabulous!* insists upon labeling *Billy* as "gay" is its certainty that this would be the first and final impression of the film by any queer viewer or sensitive straight person. Oh heck, the straight person doesn't even have to be particularly sensitive. Anytime you take a male character, be he boy or man, and transpose him into a historically feminine setting (and yes, the world of ballet has that connotation, which *Fabulous!* does not interpret as negative), anyone within the sight of it will see it the same fey way. Keep in mind that the audience's instantaneous reaction to the peculiar proceedings are expected to match those of Billy's father, and his cohorts, or the full folly of it will not take wing.

But there is even more queerness at work here. Subconsciously, there could be no gay male watching *Billy* who wouldn't be asking himself this question: Is he gay? Of course, this is our own instantaneous reaction to *Billy* being set in such a familiar place. It is also terribly important for us to know on whose side Billy will end up because we so infrequently have the opportunity to add to our numbers via an albeit small indie film, and his answer precipitates how we will judge the success or failure of his future and the film's present endeavors. Thankfully, *Billy* does not insult our gay logic in the way films like *Footloose* and *Fame* have done in the past by turning the "out" inside of a topic where we should be much more prominent and making us appear as also-rans.

Fabulous! will not tell you Billy's ultimate sexual destiny (and note that his sexual ambiguity allows this film to appear in *Fabulous!* under its "no gay male content" clause). But it will say that what distinguishes his plight is that his orientation does not (or should not) matter. For his is not really a story about sexuality, per se. It is about a boy being given the chance to be himself and not what others expect. Of course, it is also about a father's true love, like that which a boy always expects from his mother, which he hopes will be there no matter the outcome.

"Just because I like ballet doesn't mean I'm a poof, you know."

Above: Spoken by Billy Elliot (Jamie Bell) while he has his hands inside the jacket of his best friend Michael. *Right:* Billy in his female-dominated ballet class. Kobal

1963. Universal. Directed by Alfred Hitchcock. Starring Tippi Hedren, Rod Taylor, Jessica Tandy, Suzanne Pleshette, and Veronica Cartwright.

★

The basic story: A rich and beautiful San Francisco socialite and "party girl" is taken with a handsome but unimpressed lawyer whom she follows up the coast to his weekend home, which he shares with his sister and repressed mother. But she finds more than she's bargained for when all the real "chicks" in town take her arrival as an excuse to start a war against mankind.

★

Horror rarely rates high on gay favorite film lists (usually being too gory for our sensitive natures). But in the case of Hitchcock's fowl-feathered flick an exception is made. Why? First of all, aside from a few pecked-out peepers it isn't as gross as most. Second, it is unique within the Hitchcock canon (although rife with his fave mysogynist themes). Third, and possibly the most important reason why it is so irresistably gay: the master's casting of an unknown "actress" in the lead, Tippi Hedren.

Unquestionably a beauty to behold, Hedren's mannequinlike demeanor still left something to be desired by filmcrafters, but had much to delight filmgoers. Tippi, Tippi, Tippi, is it any surprise to know that you were a still model before venturing in front of a motion-picture camera? No, we think not. However, Hedren's uptight performance in *Birds* may have had as much to do with her pinched wardrobe as it did her "board stiff" acting. While the poor thing does get to wear a fancy fur twice and purchase a nightie in a brown paper bag (pretty!), she is confined to wearing a single tailored day suit for most of the film. How horrid! Yet in this pleasing pea-green get-up our trouper still manages to:

• drive sixty miles up the California coast

• steer a bathtub-sized boat across Bodega Bay

• attend dinner with a strange family (it helps that beefy Rod Taylor is serving the meat)

• sip sherry later that night with Rod's envious ex (a gravelly Suzanne Pleshette)

• rise the next day to serve cake at Rod's sister's (an effusive Veronica Cartwright) birthday party

• battle birds at same, now-be-fowled fete

• fend off more foul fowl back inside the house

• wake the next day, re-don the suit, and serve tea to Rod's tepid mother (a sour Jessica Tandy)

• smoke outside a school, and endure that song!

• defend herself from a flock of smoke- and song-hating crows, along with hordes of screaming kids!

• withstand a dressing-down in a restaurant from, among others, a rather "butch" lady birdwatcher

• trap herself in a phone booth

• sleep sitting up back at Rod's place

• pass out in an upstairs room *avec plus oiseaux*

• be dragged out of said room by the shoulder of the now-soiled testament to quality textiles

A Tippi tidbit:

For her sartorial success "underdressed," Ms. Hedren pocketed a 1963 Golden Globe for Most Promising Newcomer, but shared it with Ursula Andress and Elke Sommer. (Hmmm, wonder why they don't give out this award anymore?)

"I think you're the cause of this. I think you're evil! EVIL!!!!!!"

Above: Spoken by an enraged mother (Doreen Lang) to just-visiting Melanie Daniels (Tippi Hedren) while together in their harborside diner haven. *Left:* A *Birds* publicity shot featuring Tippi Hedren. Kobal

Boogie Nights

1997. New Line. Directed by Paul Thomas Anderson. Starring Mark Wahlberg, Burt Reynolds (AAN), Julianne Moore (AAN), John C. Reilly, Don Cheadle, Heather Graham, Luis Guzman, Philip Seymour Hoffman, William H. Macy, Alfred Molina, and Thomas Jane.

★

The basic story: During the late seventies a young man with an ample endowment becomes a "big" star during the porn industry's "golden age." But he must endure rough times as the business matures into the eighties.

★

Have you heard the rumor that all gay men at one time or another have fantasized about being porn stars? Well, you might have missed hearing it because the sound was drowned out by the same rumor about straight men. Okay, guys, what is the adult-film attraction? Basically it boils down to these three things:

getting paid *to have sex*
you are good-looking with a great bod
you possess a* large *phallus

So now what's not to understand about the gay and straight male popularity of *Boogie*—and its *long* lead, Dirk Diggler (aka Mark Wahlberg)? If this is still a dilemma, maybe it's time to get out more lesson books!

But, really, if this is not enough gay excuse to boogie the night away, try seeing it this way: sooner or later viewers should realize that they are "in bed" with director Anderson and his two-and-a-half-hour cerebral "F" session (we are hesitant to use the full four-letter word, lest it offend). Is this fornication fantasy on the part of

Fabulous!? Replay some of these homo-sexy *Boogie* scenarios and decide for yourself: the extended foreplay between Dirk and Reed Rothchild (John C. Reilly); Dirk getting *shaft*-ed in a pickup (also known as *orgasm interruptus*) about halfway into the film; the "climax" with a *shooting*, super-seventies clone-ish Thomas Jane, equating violence with the erotic; and the "cuddly" coda. Then admit that within a few minutes you're ready to "drop trou" (as is Dirk) and start over again. (Note: The only thing viewers should not repeat is Philip Seymour Hoffman's brilliant but wince-inducing role as Scotty J., the sniveling sissy subordinate.)

★

More to dance about in Boogie:

• The "steppin' out" soundtrack, which, to members of a certain age (or not!) in the gay community, should sound like music to thine ears.

• Mark Wahlberg in a Speedo is truly a sight you want to be-holding, even though by then he can't form a sentence (but who wants him talking?).

• It looks to be made of some foul-tasting synthetic, but you do get to see what all the brouhaha is about at the end of the movie!

Five more homo-sexy male couplings you may also have missed seeing:

★

Chuck Heston and Steve Boyd in *Ben-Hur* (1959)
Sean Connery and Bob Shaw in *From Russia With Love* (1963)
Chuck Bronson and John Leyton in *The Great Escape* (1963)
Guy Madison and Bob Montgomery in *Since You Went Away* (1944)
Larry Olivier and Tony Curtis in *Spartacus* (1960)

"You're not the boss of me, Jack! You're not the king of Dirk! I'm the boss of me!"

Above: Spoken in frustrated anger by Dirk Diggler (Mark Wahlberg) to his mentor, pornographer Jack Horner (Burt Reynolds). *Right:* Horner (on the left) instructing Diggler to calm down, or else. Kobal

1961. Paramount. Directed by Blake Edwards. Starring Audrey Hepburn (AAN), George Peppard, Patricia Neal, Martin Balsam, Mickey Rooney, Buddy Ebsen, Villalonga, John McGiver, Alan Reed, and Dorothy Whitney.

★

The basic story: A young New York writer—who supplements his income by being a reluctant male gigolo—befriends a kooky and emotionally immature woman. Together they find love and turn the city into a living, breathing Valentine. However, when reality sets in their expectations must change.

★

For gay blades living out in the country, is it a dream to one day move to the big city and become "the toast of the town"? This seems to be the understanding behind much of Truman Capote's motives when he penned his petite paean to a party girl (or "party boy," as it is widely believed to be at least partly autobiographical of the gay writer's own occasional odyssey in the Big Apple). *Fabulous!* agrees that leading a life fantastic has queer appeal over a ho-hum existence in the hinters. But be warned, laddies. Even in the book's close (and not in the soaking filmed version) tiny Tru reminds readers that festive days and nights don't always bring "true" happiness, and that the search could continue, unendingly, if you are looking for it in the wrong places.

But the filmed *Breakfast* is a much softer wake-up call when it comes to ringing those alarm bells. And gay fans, along with a not-so-small amount of straight female compatriots (do any straight men like this movie?) seem perfectly happy having made it into

something of a romance *Breakfast* of champions, despite Capote's crispy box of "flakes" having gotten a bit milk-mushier in the translation. But still, who could dispute the film's popularity with such lovable leads as adorable Audrey Hepburn and gorgeous George Peppard? Certainly not *Fabulous!* Further, it's eye-candy sweet for anyone who likes to look at beautiful things (what!? gay men like to look at pretty people and pretty clothes—Givenchy?! Trigere?!); an exquisite earful for those who like listening to beautiful music (frankly, if by the opening sounds of Henry Mancini's Oscar-winning "Moon River" your flesh hasn't goosed over, check for a pulse!); and a Tiffany's-bought surprise (kudos to "sales help" John McGiver) for men and women with enough imagination to think that Manhattan could really be such a playground without penalty. Ah, that it might be so!

★

However, there are a few spots in *Tiffany's* which make it sparkle just a little less than the real thing (although this shouldn't keep you from window-shopping!):

• Mickey Rooney's drippy, buck-toothed, lascivious characterization of Japanese photographer Mr. Yunioshi. Easily one of the all-time most offensive minority characters set on film. Yeech!

• The film takes liberties in reinterpreting the slightly un-PC grown-up novella: originally, it was set during World War II; Golightly was a blond-ish nineteen-year-old, Varjak was vaguely gay and *not* a gigolo; the pair's relationship was friendly but nonsexual; and it overturned the sad ending by choosing to finish Hollywood-style sweetly in the rain.

"We're alike, me and Cat. A couple of poor, nameless slobs."

Above: Spoken as part of the introductory conversation between Holly Golightly (Audrey Hepburn) and her new upstairs neighbor, writer Paul Varjak (George Peppard). *Left:* At her party, Holly receives lighted matches from both Paul (far left) and her agent, O. J. Berman (Martin Balsam). Everett

Breaking Away

1979. Twentieth Century-Fox (AAN). Directed by Peter Yates (AAN). Starring Dennis Christopher, Dennis Quaid, Daniel Stern, Jackie Earle Haley, Barbara Barrie (AAN), Paul Dooley, Robyn Douglass, and Hart Bochner.

The basic story: A group of four young male friends must contend with each other's frustrations, their families, and growing up in a small Indiana town dominated by a large college and its well-to-do transient students.

★

To gay moviegoers, homoerotic movies reveal themselves like desert watering holes for quenching desires parched by too much dry heterosexual film fare. Often, though, what we claim as "queer" oases on an endless "normal" landscape are dismissed by straights (and not a few gay men) as mere illusion. Fortunately, the *homo*-sexiness of this particular film is neither a mirage nor as shifty as the sands themselves. Actually, in the humble opinion of *Fabulous!*, *Breaking* is one if not the gay-sexiest film of all time, and here are indications of the queer inclinations to be seen in *Away:*

The Loner

Played by a spoke-slim Dennis Christopher, lean and lithe lead Dave is too shy to be himself around girls, but knows how to "playact" gallant and sensitive; he has few friends (and those he has are also "misfits"); he looks for acceptance among his peers, but ultimately chooses to go his own way (often on a bike!); he also shaves his legs, listens to opera, is learning Italian, and, for heaven's sake, owns a cat!

The Sport of Biking

On a list ranking the maschismo factor of individual sports, biking decidedly ends up on the low end of the scale (but very high on one of attraction to gay men).

The Rivalry

Dennis Quaid, shirtless in short-shorts, against Hart Bochner, the ripped rapscallion in a red Speedo. Even though the menace between these men is obvious, so, too, is the sexual chemistry.

The Distant Dad; the Doting Mom

Clearly Dad (likably played by Paul Dooley) is not as removed as some film fathers from their offshoots, but he is obviously a balance for Barbara Barrie's nearly over-sympathetic Mom with a shoulder for her son to cry on.

The "Props"

The other women in *Breaking* appear like signposts representing the last stands of heterosexuality, especially in the scene when Dave reveals his true self ("coming out") to Katherine (Robyn Douglass). Poor girl, his good manners shoulda been a clue.

If for you *Breaking* does not take home the homoerotic film prize, maybe one of these will run away with it:

★

All Quiet on the Western Front (1930, AA)
Chariots of Fire (1981, AA)
Fight Club (1999)
The Lost Boys (1987)
The Sting (1973, AA)

"No, I don't feel lucky to be alive! I feel lucky I'm not dead. There's a difference."

Above: Spoken exasperatedly by Dad (Paul Dooley) to his son Dave (Dennis Christopher). *Right: Breaking* publicity shot featuring Dennis Christopher. Kobal

1935. Universal. Directed by James Whale. Starring Boris Karloff, Colin Clive, Valerie Hobson, Elsa Lanchester, Ernest Thesiger, Gavin Gordon, Douglas Walton, and Una O'Connor.

★

The basic plot: Baron Frankenstein is coerced into reviving his "monster" by a fellow scientist, Dr. Pretorious, with the added intention that together they create for him a female mate, his "bride."

★

Awareness of something more than just what is being shown onscreen often increases a film's overall enjoyment value. In the case of *Bride*, a great deal of insider information is available, and the nature of that knowledge to those to whom it should bring the most pleasure, gay men, makes a viewing of *Bride* the perfect marriage of sights and sounds.

At a glance today, *Bride* is a surprisingly *fraidy-cat* excuse for those expecting a scary movie—what with the expectations of having that name in the title and all! (Though it should be mentioned that the film did frighten some filmgoers upon its dark, Depression-era release.) Yet underneath its *boo*-less exterior lies a wicked wonderland, and the deadpan handling of the "undead" subject, intentional on the part of gay director James Whale, is just the beginning of his *Bride*'s devilish delights.

Following up on his *Frankenstein* success, the maestro's aim was to spoof the spooky genre that had given him so much acclaim. But whether Whale was fully aware of creating a lab crowded with queer aesthetics is a matter to be tested. Fortunately, he left behind in *Bride* a filmed textbook filled with scenes of the impossibly chic, the wildly witty, and the fabulously fantastic for closer and continued gay scrutiny. Examples of Whale at his most eloquent and effete:

• The "prelude." Though some TV airings cut this concocted chat between original *Frankenstein* author Mary Shelley (Lanchester), her husband, Percy (Walton), and Lord Byron (Gordon)—what a pair of sissies!—it is definitely worth waiting to see a copy intact.

• The blind forest "friend," which was lampooned in Mel Brooks's *Young Frankenstein* (see page 176). If you don't see the scene's implicit gayness, you might want to step "out" of the forest for another look.

• The "bride." Along with help from his behind-the-*screams* crew, Whale brought the most deadly divine spouse in cinema history to life.

More "bouquets" to behold in Bride:

• Colin Clive, as Baron Frankenstein was gay, but quite unhappy with his homosexuality.

• Ernest Thesiger, as queer Dr. Pretorious, was also gay, but was said to be a most happy fellow.

• Elsa Lanchester (the Bride) was married forever to one of England's most distinguished (and closeted) actors, Charles Laughton.

• Speaking of "queenly" men, while the sexuality of Boris Karloff is not an issue (though he was English—ahem—and married five times!), that of his monstrous outsider looking for acceptance might be.

"We belong dead!"

Above: Spoken solemnly by the monster (Boris Karloff) to his bride (Elsa Lanchester) and Dr. Pretorious (Ernest Thesiger) just moments before the castle laboratory explodes. *Left:* From far left, Dr. Henry Frankenstein (Colin Clive), the bride, the monster (Boris Karloff), and Dr. Pretorious. Everett

Cabaret

1972. Allied Artists/ABC (AAN). Directed by Bob Fosse (AA). Starring Liza Minnelli (AA), Michael York, Helmut Greim, Joel Grey (AA), Fritz Wepper, Marisa Berenson, and Elisabeth Neumann-Viertel.

★

The basic story: Denizens of decadent 1930s Berlin, including a precocious singer and her bisexual lover, cavort around the city and in the place where she performs: a nightclub whose patrons and performances mirror the problematic political changes occurring just beyond its walls.

★

Far beyond being the model for the modern "narrative" musical—nevertheless, a *willkommen* distinction (and through almost every production aspect a direct ascendant of 2002's *Chicago*)—*Cabaret*, all dressed up in decadence and perversion, may more importantly be *the* cautionary tale for the gay community. As a group often at odds with itself, some gay men empathize with the emotional and ethical impact of the lives careening toward a crash inside *Cabaret* because their delusional existences bring into softly diffused light our own very possible paths to collision.

However, shining on the other side of the coin is *Cabaret*'s life-affirming spirit that Sally Bowles (Minnelli) sings to us like a siren's song. Honestly, what good is sitting all alone in your room? Not much, as far as *Fabulous!* can tell. There's also nothing wrong with coming to hear the music play, just so long as it doesn't play on, night and day, allowing the world outside to move away and maybe even against those dancing—in denial—inside the "club."

Mein herr, one really doesn't need to linger so seriously over this film, obviously intended by director Bob Fosse to be as much a serving of bittersweet sensations as a plate of *sauer* Krauts. Or was it? Why not continue to connect-the-queer-dots on this one: Did *Cabaret*, an eight-time Oscar winner, including Best Director, lose Best Picture to *The Godfather* because Francis Ford Coppola's film was stuffed with straight-shooting studs and Fosse's was too frankly full of homosexuals, bisexuals, and transsexuals? Quite likely. Interestingly, since many see gunplay as orgasmic and akin to male sexual aggression, this makes Brando's brotherhood of men still bullethole-ridden with questionable subversive sexuality. Well, the boys may have won after all!

★

The "gayest" attraction in Cabaret*:*
No summary of this movie would be complete without a further mention of Liza Minnelli. Deemed Hollywood "royalty" upon her birth to Judy Garland and Vincente Minnelli, Liza's scepter has been a lifelong burden. But in *Cabaret*, she rose triumphantly and, in doing so, became a "princess" for a group just then beginning to rise up. In the years since, we have both stood tall, but the struggles remain.

Further on Fosse:
Though long on merit, *Cabaret* comes up short with signature Fosse dance moves. But his total choreographic contribution to *Sweet Charity* (1969), starring Shirley Maclaine, Chita Rivera, and Paula Kelly, breaks the bank, especially with the numbers "Big Spender" and "Rich Man's Frug."

"We're practically living together, so if you only like boys I wouldn't dream of pestering you."

Above: Spoken rather innocently by Sally Bowles to her new housemate and soon-to-be lover, Brian Roberts (Michael York). *Right:* Sally onstage at the Kit-Kat Club, singing "Mein Herr." Everett

1980. EMI. Directed by Nancy Walker. Starring Valerie Perrine, Bruce Jenner, Steve Guttenberg, Paul Sand, Tammy Grimes, and the Village People (Alex Briley, David Hodo, Glenn Hughes, Randy Jones, Felipe Rose, and Ray Simpson).

★

The basic story: A handsome young man living in New York's Greenwich Village enlists his female fashion-model roommate to help with his fledgling songwriting career. Together they form a singing group with men gathered from their eclectic neighborhood.

★

There are gay films and then there are "gay" films. The distinction? The former has no problem stating its bent, while the latter is less honest about inclinations. Then there are "so gay" films. These are the ones so outlandish that they go beyond being simply queer, and yet still never say so. But neither do they deny it, for no one would believe it anyway. (You can call this the "sissy syndrome," a principle which befalls supposedly heterosexual interior designers and flight attendants.) Out of all the films in *Fabulous!*, it is unlikely you will find one more "so gay" than *Music.* Neither will you find one more about the gay life experience. Too deep? No, not if you can stop and think about *Music* when it was first played.

When *Music* was conceived by Jacques Morali, founder of the vastly popular disco group the Village People and their notorious "gay" conceit, he was sure that he had a winner again, and was not alone. Caftaned Allan Carr came with $10 million and brought his good fortune gained as producer of *Grease* (the biggest hit musical since *The Sound of Music*). And they thought the time was right for a couple of dancing "queens" to capitalize cinematically on the craze (after all, hadn't John Travolta and the Bee Gees just done it?). It seemed nothing could stop *Music.* But something did. Debuting (and dying) in early 1980, it had missed the wave of disco's popularity, which had peaked and plummeted the previous year, when *Music* was being made.

However, even if it had "come out" sooner it is doubtful mainstream audiences would have been ready for *Can't.* Everywhere you turn there is another "trick" or tasty treat, and much of the fun comes in watching woeful attempts at cover (if they were even trying!). *Music* even moved beyond normal camp and became an instant folderol fete *du jour.* The time necessitated the hiring of then-winning decathlete Bruce Jenner (and what a joy he was to look at!). Too bad acting wasn't like handling a pole vault! And what possible "bounty" could they have expected when they asked Nancy Walker to direct? But "quicker-picker-uppers" know the gayest parts of *Music* grab with its musical numbers, and "YMCA" (a bonanza for buff body watchers) and "Milkshake" (a novelty so carnally choreographed it begs to be seen in private heavy rotation) make this film a must-see for anyone with an appreciation for the silly and sexual.

However some songs, like "Liberation," lyrically say a little bit more by pointing out the anticipation of a community just coming out and its initial naïve sexual euphoria. To today's viewers, this tight connection to its time (pre-AIDS, post-Carter) brings out the movie's melancholy edge, and our own world's recent socio-political regression. The sight of *Music* is not so sad, though, if we can keep the promises and stop the retreat.

"I adore San Francisco! My favorite ex-husband lives there."

Above: Spoken without a hint of irony by modeling agent Sydney Channing (Tammy Grimes) to Helen Morell (June Havoc), mother of the Village People founder, Jack Morell (Steve Guttenberg). *Left:* Center, in a Princeton T-shirt and hot pants, Jack, model Samantha Simpson (Valerie Perrine), and in a midriff-T and cutoffs, her boyfriend Ron White (Bruce Jenner), surrounded by all the members of the Village People. Everett

1976. MGM. Directed by Brian DePalma. Starring Sissy Spacek (AAN), Piper Laurie (AAN), Amy Irving, William Katt, Betty Buckley, Nancy Allen, John Travolta, P.J. Soles, and Priscilla Pointer.

★

The basic story: A shy high-school coed is harassed by fellow students and mentally abused by her mother. By the time she very nearly reaches her breaking point, the young woman discovers she has ways to deal with the horrific anguish in her life, which are more powerful—and dangerous—than anyone, including herself, could have imagined.

★

We may turn a blind eye to the action being thrown around in this film—pig's blood, kitchen knives, and tampons!—but never loose sight that at the center of the flying detritus sits a character so compellingly "gay" (Carrie White, as played by a super Sissy Spacek) that it begs for her story to be redone with an all-queer cast. Alas, this may be too much to hope for. Nevertheless, what gay man growing up did not experience much of the same terrible taunting, sneering, and oh-so-hauntingly, equally ego-shattering locker-room experiences (a place so homoerotic and homophobic at the same time) as our fawning heroine? C'mon, *Fabulous!* would like to see a show of manicured hands.

Further, our feelings do not stop at mere silent sympathy for the fawn-turned-firestarter in this schlocky, but stylish shocker. We cheer loudly and generously for her skinny baby-blue-chiffon-clad butt during her devastating denouément—and, frankly, would

vote for Carrie as prom queen anytime. Why? Because deep down most gay men understand what she went through. Besides, who wouldn't want to have some kick-ass telekenetic power at their fingertips—and wouldn't high school have been a helluva nicer and prettier place for everyone if we did?

★

Carrie at her most "queer":
• Momma from hell sending our poor waif into "the closet" to ask forgiveness for allowing into her mind and speaking such unclean sexual thoughts. Now how's that as a strikingly albeit derisively gay metaphor?
• While neither may now be your type, during the sexy seventies there were no two hotter "gay" fantasy partners around than John Travolta or William Katt. (But what were we thinking, with all that hair?)

★

Carrie "ons":
• Betty Buckley, as gym teacher Miss Collins in the film, played the mother role in the unsuccessful musical stage version of this Stephen King original tale.
• Nancy Allen, once married to director DePalma, was set to play Carrie until Spacek's audition convinced him otherwise. Sorry, Nance!
• As Susan Snell, Amy Irving played opposite her real-life mom, Priscilla Pointer (Mrs. Snell).

Carrie-d "away":
Dressed to Kill (1981) is yet another stylish DePalma thriller and a gay favorite mainly because its star Angie Dickinson dresses (and undresses) quite chicly for the short amount of time she's onscreen!

"He took me, with the stink of filthy roadhouse whiskey on his breath, and I liked it. I liked it!"

Above: Spoken by Margaret White (Piper Laurie) in an impassioned confessional to her daughter, Carrie White (Sissy Spacek). *Right:* Carrie and her date, Tommy Ross (William Katt), just after being named king and queen of the prom. Everett

2002. Miramax (AA). Directed by Rob Marshall (AAN). Starring Renee Zellwegger (AAN), Catherine Zeta-Jones (AA), Richard Gere, Queen Latifah (AAN), John C. Reilly (AAN), Christine Baranski, Taye Diggs, and Lucy Liu.

★

The basic story: A young married woman kills her adulterous lover and is sent to jail to await trial. While incarcerated, she meets others in similar straits, including an accused double murderess; becomes friendly with the matron; and secures a fast-talking lawyer. Throughout her days behind bars, she passes the time by dreaming of her as yet unrealized career as an entertainer.

★

In the year 2001, word began buzzing about that the sound of the musical had returned from a decades-long silence. And the cause? The release of Baz Luhrmann's bombastic *Moulin Rouge.* But had the praise been shouted too loudly for a film that was perceived by many as unable to sustain itself beyond being a tuneful but one-note novelty? *The comment will no doubt get fans humming.* By the following year, however, voices again were heard to herald the comeback of what some really thought was a closed subject in Hollywood. But this time nary a sour note was sung, for nearly everyone agreed that the long, *long*-awaited arrival of *Chicago* was something to sing out loud about.

However, let's get something "straight," *Chicago* is not in *Fabulous!* because it is a recent gay favorite (and a huge one at that!). The odds are this "razzler-dazzler," in the parlance of character Billy Flynn (Richard Gere), would be included in editions of *Fabulous!* years from now. But while *Chicago* is definitely "our kinda" film, to include it there must be more good reasons. Fortunately, there are. Inside and out, *Chicago* is a film full of gay "sense and sensibility" with the bonus of aesthetic updating for twenty-first-century tastes. How does *Chicago* do this? First, by separating the inherent "fantasy" aspects of musicals, the numbers, into their own parts away from the supposed "reality." (Unfortunately, this division may not be possible in all subsequent genre revivals.) Then by giving ample glimpses of "T&A" to entice heterosexual men (a key contingent missing from many past musicals) while not demeaning the ever-present feminine power factor—starting with the female jailhouse setting—which never crosses the line into total anti-male territory. Simultaneously, gay men enjoy the glamorous touches throughout knowing that we were the ones behind the scenes bringing all the pieces together. Voila!

★

Who and what got lost in the Chicago *transfer:* Obviously unable to do it justice, the film *Chicago* forgoes a great surprise stage revelation with reporter Mary Sunshine (played onscreen by Christine Baranski). But it's the perfect reason to catch the show on tour!

Not all gay men love musicals (or kittens, chocolate martinis, and disco!). But here are five females who try their darnedest, convincing those who don't to swing along:

★

Ann-Margret in *Bye, Bye Birdie* (1963)
Doris Day in *The Pajama Game* (1957)
Shirley Jones in *The Music Man* (1962)
Ethel Merman in *Call Me Madam* (1953)
Ann Miller in *Kiss Me Kate* (1953)

"Don't you wanna take my picture?"

Above: Spoken hurtfully by Roxie Hart (Renee Zellweger) to reporters departing her just-concluded murder trial. *Left:* Zellweger flanked by assembled male dancers in the fantasy number "Roxie." Kobal

Clueless

1995. Paramount. Directed by Amy Heckerling. Starring Alicia Silverstone, Stacey Dash, Brittany Murphy, Paul Rudd, Dan Hedaya, Donald Faison, Breckin Meyer, Justin Walker, Jeremy Sisto, and Elisa Donovan.

★

The basic story: After successfully making a match between two of their teachers, two well-intentioned, pretty high-school girls endeavor to make over a recently transferred "clueless" female classmate. While all does not go according to plan, the main protagonist embarks on a journey of self-discovery and ends up happier and more respected than when she began.

★

Yes, this is a movie for teenagers. No, that does not mean adult gay men who like it are juvenile (maybe a little bit schoolgirlish, but not juvenile). However, since *Clueless* makes it very clear at the outset that its lead character, Cher (now how's that name for a queer way to attract an audience?), has three main objectives in life—shopping, makeovers, and boys—is it any wonder why even as grown-ups we gay men are tempted to partake of the fun in her playground?

Furthermore, *Clueless* is more than just a cute two-hour recess period on the rather facile pleasures of some young females (and gay men). Quickly it should become apparent—unless *you* happen to be clueless—that the film has something more on its mind than boys (not that there's anything wrong with that). *Clueless* is actually a clever classroom romp through the life of a "dish" nowhere near as ditzy as first imagined, and whose inclusive attitude is the real reason why gay men have enrolled (that and the "literal" excuse we tell our cine-

matically superior friends: *Clueless* is a modern reworking of the Jane Austen classic *Emma* and far more entertaining to watch than the more-faithful Gwyneth Paltrow film version from the following year).

Clueless, like the closet of every Beverly Hills babe with access to daddy's bank account, has even more up its sleeve for "fashionable" viewers. Director Amy Heckerling has successfully outfitted a young screen heroine (and gay person in designer disguise) who shows us that the world really can be a nicer place to live in—if you devote enough time to hair, makeup, and wardrobe. Heckerling also introduces students of the movies to a rarity: a secondary but complimentary gay character, Christian Stovitz (Justin Walker). Though rather too swaggeringly presented at the start, he is the only male to perform a physical act of heroism later onscreen. Bravo! But more endearingly, while everyone except Cher already knows that he is a "cakeboy," she is only upset at her own ineptitude upon hearing the news and not at finding out the true sexuality of her onetime dream date. Cher even goes on to express appreciation for the knowledge he brings to her of fine art and film. Added up, these little extra-credit gay touches place *Clueless* high on our film honor roll.

The "Most Likely to Succeed" from the class of Clueless: While Alicia Silverstone (Cher) has not yet graduated to the higher levels anticipated with this surprise sleeper hit, the basic makeover principles seem to have been taken to heart by Brittany Murphy (Tai Frasier), who is now almost too beautifully unrecognizable from her former frumpy self. Go Brittn'y! Go Brittn'y!

"Ms. Stoeger, my plastic surgeon doesn't want me doing any activity where balls fly at my nose."

Above: Spoken "cluelessly" by Amber Princess Mariens (Elisa Donovan) to her gym teacher, Coach Millie Stoeger (Julie Brown), during tennis practice. *Right:* Cher Horowitz (Alicia Silverstone) and her half brother by marriage, Josh Lucas (Paul Rudd). Everett

1944. Universal-International. Directed by Robert Siodmak. Starring Maria Montez, Jon Hall, Sabu, Mary Nash, Edgar Barrier, Lois Collier, Lon Chaney Jr., Moroni Olsen, and Samuel S. Hinds.

★

The basic story: Twin sisters are separated at birth. One becomes the "evil" ruler of an island that worships cobras(!) and engages in ritual sacrifices. The "good" sister first finds out that she has a sibling, then becomes aware of her sibling's lethal activities and sneaks onto the island. A struggle for power ensues.

★

Part of the Introduction to *Fabulous!* was a mention of the assumed tight connection between "camp" films and the gay filmgoer. Since it was brief we will elaborate. While many gay men appreciate "camp," too often it is thought that these are the only types of movies we love. True, many of our favorites are campy, but that is just by happenstance; we do not make it a habit of seeking out only those with this silly added value (and it should be mentioned that nearly every pre-sixties film now holds some "camp" elements). It also bears repeating that not all gay men like the movies. This is important to note, because "camp" films represent moviemaking gone awry. For them to come off correctly they need to be juxtaposed with those resulting in better-quality viewing—and an awareness of filmdom's highs and lows usually comes from being an ardent movie lover.

This brings us to the simple *Fabulous!* rule for what *turns* a movie into "camp": the accidental clashing of good and/or bad talent or timing which renders the finished film affected or artificial. For a movie to be considered honest "camp" it shouldn't try to be so deliberately. Obvious intent makes the film into a spoof, which isn't really the same thing.

Fabulous! is now happy to present a prime representative of the hokum Hollywood has poorly or overly produced, marvelously miscast, and dutifully but dumbly directed. Theoretically, most everything seemed all right with *Cobra* at the start (a film of such goofy charms it begs to be coaxed out of its basket for a look-see). The crew even included one-day Oscar-nominated Richard Siodmak as director and one-day Oscar-winner Richard Brooks as script co-writer. What went wonderfully wrong? Well, while everyone must share in the blame for this Technicolor travesty—including a hairy-chested Jon Hall and tiny, tanned Sabu!—the real credit should be laid at the too-well-made, high-heel-sandaled feet of a performer as egregious as she was exotic, Maria Montez (in her dual role as Tollea and Nadia!).

A big star in forties escapist fare despite her unavoidable accent and unmistakable lack of acting ability, Montez is a beloved "camp" icon and *Cobra* is certainly one of the best examples of what floats to the top of the Hollywood cesspool. But neither Montez nor *Cobra* sits on their throne alone. Here are five more "queens" and key films to this kingdom full of ridiculous riches:

★

Joan Collins in *The Opposite Sex* (1956)
Zsa Zsa Gabor in *Queen of Outer Space* (1958)
Hedy Lamarr in *White Cargo* (1942)
Jayne Mansfield in *The Girl Can't Help It* (1956)
Carmen Miranda in *The Gang's All Here* (1943)

"Gif me the cobra jool."

Above: Spoken by "good" twin sister, Nadja (Maria Montez), asking for the symbol of power. *Left: Cobra* publicity shot featuring Montez and Jon Hall (Ramu). Kobal

Dangerous Liaisons

1988. Warner Bros. (AAN). Directed by Stephen Frears. Starring Glenn Close (AAN), John Malkovich, Michelle Pfeiffer (AAN), Swoosie Kurtz, Keanu Reeves, Mildred Natwick, and Uma Thurman.

★

The basic story: A scheming marquise enlists her one-time lover, a vicomte, to engage in a game of sexual temptation with a chaste young woman who is set to marry the marquise's ex-husband. Meanwhile, the vicomte has plans of his own, which upset those of the marquise.

★

The overall sense of promiscuity that pervades gay culture has created the impression—for better or worse—that the greatest part of our population is very savvy when it comes to the "ins and outs" of sex. Further, if having sex was something of a competition, we, with our supposed predilection for "game playing," "playing around," and "playing the field," would be expected to win nearly all of the time. Whether this sexual reputation has been justly earned or unjustly dropped at our feet unfortunately doesn't matter. The stamp has been placed and we must bear the brunt of it as best we can. However, this brings us to the dirty deeds on full display in *Dangerous*, the intriguing intercourse taking place among its titular characters, and why to some gay men it does seem so fornicatingly familiar.

With bosoms aplenty at every turn, *Dangerous* cleaved its way into a milieu already top heavy with pumped stars. But getting a busty Glenn Close near to film fare offered by a chesty Arnold Schwarzenegger or Sylvester Stallone was hardly the intended marketing position for this movie. Since everything was already so "big" in film at the time, it seemed that director Stephen Frears (*Prick Up Your Ears*, 1987) had the right idea by, one assumes, expecting to see a much "slimmer" audience show up in attendance. For whom else could Frears have had in mind to watch—a coy Keanu Reeves and the powdered-paleness of John Malkovich as a character weakened by his manipulations and passionate power struggles—than contemporary fops who understood the sexual shenanigans and desperately needed an antidote for the steroidally enlarged pictures that had recently overcrowded theaters? Doubtless this film, too, so tightly bound and morally loose at the same time, would prove far too peevishly perverted to bring in a straight male demographic. Nor is there a better period film available to show the fragrant differences in the flagrantly different tastes between our two persuasions. Period.

★

A Dangerous *question:*
Did having Madame de Tourvel (Michelle Pfeiffer) either keep her corset on ("safe") or remove it ("unsafe") make these undergarments into symbols of chastity *and* physically symbolic of condoms in a movie that fully implies that sex can be lethal and was made during the height of the AIDS health scare?

Liaisons *we meet again:*
Dangerous was filmed once in 1960, and as *Valmont* in 1989 (with Colin Firth, Annette Bening, and Meg Tilly), and again just as the story basis for *Cruel Intentions* (1999), the film which brought together now-married stars, and recent gay favorites, Reese Witherspoon and Ryan Phillippe.

"One does not applaud the tenor for clearing his throat."

Above: Spoken beratingly by the Marquise de Merteuil (Glenn Close) to the Vicomte de Valmont (John Malkovich) as they discuss details of their ongoing sex games. *Right: Dangerous* publicity shot featuring Close and Malkovich. Everett

1933. MGM. Directed by George Cukor. Starring Marie Dressler, John Barrymore, Wallace Beery, Jean Harlow, Lionel Barrymore, Lee Tracy, Edmund Lowe, Billie Burke, Madge Evans, and Jean Hersholt.

★

The basic story: A married woman with social ambitions arranges to host a dinner party for visiting dignitaries. But prior to its commencement, her guests go through various stages of tumult and threaten its success.

★

If you try hosting a nice dinner party (in honor of visiting VIPs) without getting full cooperation from guests—and can still pull it off—see if that doesn't win you the admiration of any gay man who's attempted the very same (and most of us have!). You definitely have the esteem of *Fabulous!*, which feels that proper party planning is one of the hardest jobs on the planet, especially if you can't get the right stamps to color coordinate with your invitations or the right preparations to make edibles pleasing to the eye.

However, the hostess with the leastest support—Millicent Jordan (Billie Burke)—isn't the only character in *Eight* who deserves a medal for her elegant efforts. (Festive frustrations just happen to make her the most gay sympathetic.) Actually, *Dinner* is quite the winning gathering when it comes to serving audiences choice bits by a chic-and-sour cast of characters drawn right out of a drawing room (though clever film foxes will note an actual meal is never fed to the mink-trimmed crowd). But readers themselves may lose a bit of their appetites when they discover that this silver-platter entrée, so acclaimed today, won not a single film prize upon its presentation to poor Depression-era patrons, who were literally starving for this kind of sophisticated treat. Alas, that was because *Eight* was timed too early when it came to being in the right place to pick up awards. The people over at the just-five-years-young Academy had not yet worked in all the many categories which "Oscar watchers" (hmmm, anyone you know?) have now come to expect. In particular, "supporting" had not yet been named a category for actors. This left the pieces in *Dinner* without any pie to share. (This Oscar oversight was rectified in 1936; the first winners were Gale Sondergaard for *Anthony Adverse* and Walter Brennan for *Come and Get It!*)

★

The gayest Dinner *guests:*
• Jean Harlow as Kitty Packard. Though this was not the first time she lit up cameras, Harlow's famously biased-dressed part in *Eight* became the most iconic for both her and films when her "platinum" presence forever turned the screen "silver."
• Jean Hersholt as Jo Stengel. Oscar followers know his name well, but not his face. *Dinner* is a chance to actually see the charitable man for whom the Academy named their prestigious "humanitarian" award.
• Marie Dressler as Carlotta Vance. Take the most rough-and-tumble, least glamorous woman you can find, give her an Oscar (as Tugboat Annie in *Min and Bill*, 1930), and you've got some idea of the unusual star you'd be up against. The surprise is that in her day, crossing over from silents into talkies, Marie was very large—and still in charge. Hollywood has yet to come close to filling her oversized personality.

"I was reading a book the other day . . ."

Above: Spoken blithely by Kitty Packard (Jean Harlow) to Carlotta Vance (Marie Dressler) while they are both on their way into dinner. *Left:* Kitty in the bedroom of the home she shares with her loutish husband, Dan Packard (Wallace Beery). Everett

Doctor Zhivago

1965. MGM (AAN). Directed by David Lean (AAN). Starring Omar Sharif, Julie Christie, Rod Steiger, Alec Guinness, Tom Courtenay (AAN), Geraldine Chaplin, Siobhan McKenna, Ralph Richardson, and Rita Tushingham.

★

The basic story: The life of a Russian doctor and poet is played out against a backdrop of revolution, poverty, family obligations, passion, and his enduring love for a tragic woman.

★

Gay men are often singled out for their ability to make things pretty *and* for their appreciation of the things in life which already are, such as flowers, fallen snow, and the occasional fox-edged pink traveling suit. Imagine the ecstasy felt among gay men in finding these things and much, *much* more in just one film.

For anyone who's ailing over the world's lack of loveliness—and isn't that a favorite cry of ours?—*Doctor* is a sure tonic to cure the beauty blues. But be sure to give yourself extra time on the road to finding life's most ravishing things, for the beautiful bounty lavished along this trip may be too tedious for some to endure. Dear *Doctor*! It's nearly three-and-a-half hours long! However, hop on board if you like your movies played out, literally and figuratively, in front of your very eyes. (*Zhivago* seems to have a thing for traveling, as trekking about by locomotive or on foot is the film's favorite way to pass the time.)

Though it is possibly too much for some to tolerate, *Zhivago* is an enduring and exemplary example of what gives us all reason to see movies, and particularly what makes gay men look at director David Lean and his work with such high regard. As an executor of some of moviedom's most exquisite work, Sir David has been extended honorary membership in our club (a group with the greatest esteem for eye-popping aesthetics, and *Zhivago* pops them out regularly). But the question of his sexuality, which, mind you, has never really been at issue, does give those who believe that only gay men can make something lovely to look at something to think about when watching his signature grand vistas on full display in *Doctor*. (Note that the small screen can surely kill the experience and render this point moot.)

But bear in mind that Lean was not alone in the creation of his crown jewel of cinematic compositions. It took a whole invisible village of people behind the scenes to help make his vision clear, and among the unseen in *Doctor* are his cinematographer Freddie Young, production designer John Box, costumer Phyllis Dalton, and composer Maurice Jarre (all of whom won Oscars for their good *Doctor*'s work).

Lean is also far from being the sole straight director who has caught our eyes with their ways with the camera, and here are five gruff gents (and a film) with a genteel touch:

★

John Huston's *Moulin Rouge* (1952)
Joshua Logan's *Sayonara* (1957)
Sir Carol Reed's *Oliver!* (1968)
George Stevens's *A Place in the Sun* (1951)
Orson Welles's *The Magnificent Ambersons* (1942)

"You, my dear, are a slut!"

Above: Spoken by Komarovsky (Rod Steiger) as his concubine, Lara Antipova (Julie Christie), tries to end their illicit affair. *Right:* Yuri Zhivago (Omar Sharif) lighting Christmas tree candles with his intended, Tonya (Geraldine Chaplin), while being shadowed by Lara. (Note Lean's use of shading to differentiate between the "virtuous" [light] and the "tainted" [dark] female.) Everett

Double Indemnity

1944. Paramount (AAN). Directed by Billy Wilder (AAN). Starring Barbara Stanwyck (AAN), Fred Mac-Murray, Edward G. Robinson, Porter Hall, Jean Heather, and Tom Powers.

★

The basic story: An insurance salesman falls for a married woman who entices him to murder her husband for his money and her love.

★

To understand the gay attraction to this classic of heterosexual entertainment, some points should be made emphatically at the start. First, while *Double* is atypical of our faves, it is still a superlative film that anyone of any persuasion can love. Second, who says *Double* is such a straight movie? Not *Fabulous!* To help you see the gayness in *Double*, *Fabulous!* will match and compare it in six ways against another noted "straight" film classic from the time, *Casablanca.*

The Action

In *Indemnity:* Players use sex as "weapons," and the victim is *pushed* from the back of a slow-moving train!
In *Casablanca:* Players are focused entirely in front of a World War II backdrop.
The queer results: Since war is a "man's" game, the boys definitely choose to play with *Double.*

The Actors

In *Indemnity:* MacMurray plays an insurance salesman whose biggest worry is an actuary (Robinson).
In *Casablanca:* Bogart plays a nightclub owner who deals with nightly nefariousness.

The queer results: With the worst thing that could happen being a paper cut, the boys hire Fred (and *Double*).

The Actresses

In *Indemnity:* Stanwyck is saucy and *saph*-isticated.
In *Casablanca:* Bergman's "notorious" lovelife labels her a definite lady for the men.
The queer results: The boys go with the doll from *Double*, because we sleep in the same bed.

The Scripts

In *Indemnity:* The lines are so laden with sexual innuendo you need to smoke and shower afterward.
In *Casablanca:* The dialogue is dishy, but campier than it is carnal.
The queer results: Sex sells, so the boys buy *Double.*

The Interplay

In *Indemnity:* Cat and mouse.
In *Casablanca:* Man and woman.
The queer results: You need to ask?

The Fade-out

In *Indemnity:* Fred and Barbara succumb to bullets.
In *Casablanca:* Bogart strolls off with Claude Rains.
The queer results: Yes, in this instance, Bogey's exit gaily gets our vote.

★

The Final Gay Outcome

Five out of six times, *Double* gets caught queerly with its pants down, making it and our side the clear champ.

"I wonder if you wonder."

Above: Spoken by a soon-to-be-duped insurance salesman Walter Neff (Fred MacMurray) to duplicitous Phyllis Dietrichson (Barbara Stanwyck) early in their devious relationship. *Left:* Phyllis and Walter discuss insurance coverage, and more. Kobal

Dumbo

1941. Walt Disney. Directed by Ben Sharpsteen. Featuring the voices of Herman Bing (Ringmaster), Billy Bletcher (Clown), Edward Brophy (Timothy Q. Mouse), Jim Carmichael (Crow), Cliff Edwards (Jim Crow), Verna Felton (Matriarch), and Sterling Holloway (Mr. Stork). (Note: Dumbo does not have a speaking voice in the film, nor does his mother.)

★

The basic story: A mother elephant anxiously awaits the "arrival" of her newborn. But when the baby appears, everyone is shocked by his appearance, and he is shunned (except by momma). Banished outside his home, the youngster soon discovers that he does indeed have something to contribute, and is eventually welcomed back.

★

"Straight from heaven up above, here is a baby for you to love."

When filmmakers make family fare, they usually have just two objectives in mind: to attract kids with colorfully done yet easy-to-understand stories that do not bore parents and, most important, to not offend by being too controversial. Curiously, a very common story line used by children's film producers makes accomplishing the noncontroversial part almost impossible. That is, if anyone knew what was happening. But it seems many do not (or, as some would venture, if aware they seem not to care!).

Fabulous! is talking about the "fairy" tale favorite subject of "fitting in," which is such a recurrent theme in so many kiddy classics, you'd think by now mom and dad would have gotten the story "straight." But thankfully, they have not. Because if they did, gay men might never have seen this baby-sized gem of a movie.

Of course, while the personality traits (let alone sexuality) of any one person are hardly defined at the preadolescent stage, few can say as adults that they don't recall experiencing some degree of "missed" fit. Gay men seem especially aware of having felt ostracized as a small fry. This is what makes the story of *Dumbo*, the infant elephant with the very large ears that make him "different," sound fairly familiar. In fact, scene for scene, it is almost a too-close animated allegory of the often tragic, sometimes comic, and hopefully triumphant circumstances that all gay youths go through, including the adoring mother, befriending known enemies of his kind (a mouse and performing "black" birds), early instances of bad makeup and drag, and the ability to become a high-flying hero with what others see only as a handicap.

Whether or not Mickey expected or intended this to happen, it seems that quite a few members of his Mouseketeers Club might be sharing dual membership in our own organization. Repeat: might be. This is just a partial list of five whose cards could be carrying quite the telling scent:

★

Grumpy, a dwarf in *Snow White* (1936)
Kronk, the muscled footman
in *The Emperor's New Groove* (2000)
Peter, the boy from Neverland in *Peter Pan* (1953)
Timon, the meerkat in *The Lion King* (1994)
White Rabbit, the neurotic bunny in
Alice in Wonderland (1951)

Above: Spoken poetically by Mr. Stork (voice of Sterling Holloway) to Mrs. Jumbo. *Right:* Dumbo and his friend Timothy Q. Mouse "fly" in for a landing at the circus grounds. Everett

1994. Touchstone. Directed by Tim Burton. Starring Johnny Depp, Martin Landau (AA), Sarah Jessica Parker, Patricia Arquette, Jeffrey Jones, G. D. Spradlin, Vincent D'Onofrio, Bill Murray, Lisa Marie, and George "The Animal" Steele.

★

The basic story: The biopic of an ambitious filmmaker who made unwittingly bad, below grade B movies; his friends and actors; and the man's passion for wearing women's clothing.

★

For lovers of movie minutiae and trivia-packed pursuits (hmmm, who could that be?) this "outsider" film is an "insider" on four gay cinematic counts:

Styl-Ed!

It would seem that a black-and-white film wouldn't normally attract the attention of such a "colorful" bunch of guys. But indeed it did (as a great many gray-toned pictures in the past have, too). Besides, it was director Burton's deliberate attempt to make his film look as authentically fifties B-picturized as possible, and, in this instance, hewing it with a rainbow would have made his *Ed* too modern and then far less a queer curiosity. (Another piece of *Wood* construction to ponder: at $18 million, director Burton spent more on this film than the original man did on his entire work output combined!)

Subject-Ed!

A quirky behind-the-scenes look into the life of a queerish behind-the-eight-ball director: What's not for a gay man to love? Further, the subject is definitely rosy when it comes to flowery and factual bits being strewn all over *Ed*: his passion for angora, his good friend Bunny, much transvestitism, and Vampira (played slitheringly by waistless wonder Lisa Marie).

Direct-Ed!

Director Tim Burton, a modern movie iconoclast, has amazing appeal to many gay men. While this may surprise those who expect us to be cinema classicists, it is not so shocking if you appreciate that in his own ways Burton's weird works (and oddly enough *Ed* may be his most humane) are a witty wink to all film lovers, and that they evoke a "sensibility" which is, while not necessarily flaming, flamboyant to say the least, beginning with the "twee" *Pee-wee's Big Adventure* (1985). (Further, any man who would make it a point to find parts for a legendary screen beauty, Sylvia Sidney, will forever be a gay favorite.)

Starr-Ed!

As one of Hollywood's late-eighties "new breed" actors, Depp distinguished himself from his peers by stepping up to the plate and hitting a gay home run with his foppish-fair looks combined with a laid-back sexual attitude—and can you believe our affair started way back with his very first film, *Nightmare on Elm Street* (1984)? But it is his startling presence in a tight sweater set, black skirt, and ankle-strap shoes that makes his *Wood* appearance—from four and counting for director Burton—the most *out*-standing of all his many ambi-sexy screen performances.

"This is the most restricting coffin I've ever been in; I can't even move my arms!"

Above: Spoken by Bela Lugosi (Martin Landau) to a funeral parlor owner who'd hoped to have the horror star's endorsement. *Left:* In a scene re-created from the actual Wood film original *Glen or Glenda?* are Dolores Fuller (Sarah Jessica Parker) and Ed Wood (Johnny Depp). Kobal

Election

1999. Paramount. Directed by Alexander Payne. Starring Matthew Broderick, Reese Witherspoon, Chris Klein, and Jessica Campbell.

★

The basic story: A schoolteacher is determined to prevent an overachieving but somewhat underhanded female student from winning the election of class president by recruiting the most popular boy in school—a handsome, unassuming jock—as her opponent. Making matters more complicated, upon losing her girlfriend to her brother, the boy's lesbian sister also decides to run.

★

Upon its quiet opening, *Election* appeared like a long shot for attracting any sizable audience attention. But it ended up a winner with viewers—and critics—and a clear front runner with gay constituents as one of the friendliest films in years. This "candidate" got queen-sized support because it did not insult our intelligence by pandering with a campaign handshake. Instead, *Election* seemed to embrace gayness as a full partner of its whole agenda, and, in a significant aspect of the film, a lesbian is incorporated, not as a throwaway but as an integral member of the "family." For gay men who had grown too used to being inserted into recent films just as relief from "real men"—and hardly a revolution from earlier token roles of timidity—it was a refreshing sight to see.

Skirting around the "no gay male content" clause with a gay female also allows *Election* to enter *Fabulous!*, but it is not the only queer thing on its ballot. In many ways, this black comedy and instant classic, from its subversive bent to its sympathetic and not-so

characters, is painted "pink" all over. One gay way to see this is by taking a look at the three representative leads in *Election*, and see where each stands on "queer" issues:

Candidate #1: Matthew Broderick

Broderick, for the edification of those outside the community, is a gay man's favorite in the boy-next-door category, and has had this mate- and date-able quality since first appearing in *War Games* (1983). Other examples: Robert Morse, Chris O'Donnell, and Jake Gyllenhaal.

Candidate #2: Chris Klein

Klein is the kind of modern young male star whose buffed-out body would seem the primary gay attraction, but it is secondary to his "I'm okay with that" attitude toward his queer fan base. A definite jock type not strapped to old ways of thinking. Other examples: Tab Hunter, Jan-Michael Vincent, and Shawn Hatosy.

Candidate #3: Reese Witherspoon

In *Election*, Witherspoon plays the kind of snittish character (Tracy Flick) everyone would like to trip up, including gay men, even though as the perfectionist in an imperfect world her plight is akin to our own similar *daze* in school. Further, Reese appears cast in the same sweet mold from which we get many of our favorite female stars and seems destined to go the gay way of Doris Day, Debbie Reynolds, Sally Field, and Sandra Bullock.

★

The *Election* winner:

Everyone!

"And thank you, God, for what I've been told is a large penis."

Above: Spoken in voice-over by Paul Metzler (Chris Klein) while thinking of his last year in high school. *Right:* Tracy Enid Flick (Reese Witherspoon) confronting her class presidential opponent, Paul, in the school's offices. Kobal

1958. Twentieth Century-Fox. Directed by Kurt Neumann. Starring David Hedison, Patricia Owens, Vincent Price, Herbert Marshall, and Kathleen Freeman.

★

The basic story: A scientist at work on matter transference accidentally traps himself along with a common housefly in his conveyance machine. When reconfigured in the "receiving" machine, he finds that the genetics of his body and that of the fly have been crossed, leaving him a horrible mutation of man and insect. He also realizes that there is a fly with the reverse physical characteristics, and must find it in order to save his own life.

★

At a glance, there is nothing that seems overtly "gay" about this movie. In fact, many of its so-campy elements seem to fly in the face of what *Fabulous!* says should be found in a film to give it swishy status: it is science fiction (not a traditionally gay favorite category) and it does not have any queer-preferred stars. But like the little flit for whom it is named, getting the gayness of *The Fly* is almost impossible with your first swipe. A person has to return to this movie and look more closely before coming upon all the fabulous queer stuff in store, and here is what you will find that has the most unavoidable gay appeal:

• a handsome hubby with a God complex and sexy gray hair at his temples (who, unfortunately, becomes a not-so-hot man—with a gruesome fly head!)
• a pretty wife (Owens) with a pretty wardrobe, and a glass-shattering scream (a queer must in fifties sci-fi)
• a bookish son oddly fond of catching flies
• a brother-in-law (Price) oddly fond of his brother's wife
• a doubtful maid with a heavy hand (played by classic gay-fave character actress Kathleen Freeman)
• a doubtful investigator with a heavy heart (played by "old school" gay-fave actor Herbert Marshall)
• a dematerialized pet pussycat, named Dandello! (who is rematerialized, but in voice only: Meow!)
• meals for mutants, made of milk laced with whiskey
• a fly with a very handsome scientist's head
• a hungry spider and a very sticky web

★

But there is something more queer you might notice about *Fly.* Because films of this kind are often considered rather too silly, some discerning gay viewers choose not to regard it worthily and poo-poo the very many who do. *Fabulous!* realizes that some films are indiscriminate, but does not like to discriminate itself. Besides, *The Fly* is really terribly chi-chi for sci-fi, thanks to Cinemascope, Owens's sublime *ensembs*, and its consideration as one of the very best of the genre (and you know we love top status!). So how beneath one can it be?

Truthfully, sci-fi only rarely finds its way onto our film gaydar, but enough have to note five more here and a reason why we watch:

★

Farrah Fawcett in *Logan's Run* (1976)
A "younger" Harrison Ford in *Blade Runner* (1982)
Anne Francis's sapphire mini in *Forbidden Planet* (1956)
The "spaceship" in *When Worlds Collide* (1951)
Antibodies on Raquel Welch in *Fantastic Voyage* (1966)

"Help me! Help me-e-e-e!"

Above: Spoken in desperation by scientist Andre Delambre (David Hedison) as the mutated fly-man caught in a web with an approaching spider. *Left:* Loving wife Helene Delambre (Patricia Owens) on the stairway to her scientist-husband's laboratory, quite distraught over his recent disfiguration. Kobal

Funny Girl

1968. Columbia (AAN). Directed by William Wyler. Starring Barbra Streisand (AA), Omar Sharif, Walter Pidgeon, Kay Medford (AAN), Anne Francis, Lee Allen, Mae Questel, Gerald Mohr, and Frank Faylen.

★

The basic story: The musical biopic of legendary entertainer Fanny Brice, beginning with her days starting out in vaudeville through her run as a Ziegfeld Follies star and doomed marriage to gambler Nick Arnstein.

★

There is nothing "funny" about the way many gay men feel about this "girl": *Oh, how they love her so!* But though some boys seem way too fond of a film that now, in retrospectacular fashion, has supremely silly bits, the relationship began well before the film came out in 1968, still stands today, and is a testament to the kind of undying devotion any girl can expect from a guy—*but only if he's gay!*

Of course, for the film's star, Barbra Streisand, our loyalty is something she has counted on ever since becoming someone to watch out for in the early sixties. Noted for our ability to pick up on the "latest" and "newest," gay men—fortunate enough to have seen her back then—knew the "girl from Brooklyn" had what it takes from the beginning. But more than that, and most meaningful to anyone who ever felt like an outsider, was the fact that the rise of this "ugly duckling" gave us all the feeling that we too could become "swans." And so Streisand did. To become not just a star but a movie star (and fervid Babs fans should understand the difference). This brings us back to why, for a group favoring "reel" life twisted tales, gay men find *Girl*, with its "star-is-born-story-within-a-story," so irresistible.

But now about some of those "silly" bits as ascribed earlier. *Funny Girl* came along on the very last notes of the glory days of the musical. Ironically, and though it was a success, many of the gay-goofiest things about this film occur because they hark hokily back to those early days. The most memorable being the number "His Love Makes Me Beautiful," which, most interestingly, is secondarily directed by Herbert Ross and not William Wyler. Speaking of which, Wyler's absence is felt at other *queer* times, like when Streisand, an actress whose only constant criticism is that she needs reigning in, was allowed to run too free about the film: on a pier and, later, with a spade in hand. However, these are just the campier aspects of an otherwise class-act film which has at least one classic "gay" movie scene: the magnificent finale of Streisand singing "My Man" (which begs to be seen widescreen, or else you miss the famous fingertips!).

"To me, when a person's a stranger they should act a little strange."

Above: Spoken maternally by Rose Brice (Kay Medford) to her rising star daughter, Fanny (Barbra Streisand), about the latter's almost too-charming surprise suitor, Nick Arnstein (Omar Sharif). *Right:* Fanny seated and feeling somewhat uncomfortable in Arnstein's private dining room. Kobal

1947. Twentieth Century-Fox. Directed by Joseph Mankiewicz. Starring Gene Tierney, Rex Harrison, George Sanders, Edna Best, Vanessa Brown, Anna Lee, Robert Coote, Natalie Wood, Isobel Elsom, and Victoria Horne.

★

The basic story: A recent widow, her daughter, a housekeeper, and a dog move into a seaside cottage inhabited by the ghost of its former occupant. At first an awkward alliance is formed between the "man" and the woman, but it soon grows into something more.

★

Early in life, many gay men often begin to "make things up" in order to fit into the straight world. Fortunately, we also learn that "making believe" can be a good thing, and find that if you have an imagination it can take you places far beyond your "normal" reach.

However, just because some gay men like fantasizing (and are frequently good at it) are we always fantasy fans? No. But we can be if the dream is as beautifully realized as it is in *Ghost*, an elegantly ethereal film with a solid cast, including an especially touching Gene Tierney, a sexy Rex Harrison, and, as a children's book author who writes under the name Uncle Neddy, a weasely (as per usual) George Sanders; a firm crew, which includes some of composer Bernard Herrmann's and cinematographer Charles Lang's best work; and a soundly spiritual but far from frightening premise: *believing in the unbelievable* (which shows us that love and relationships need not always have clear reasoning or rhyme or be typically defined to be valid).

Over the years, too, even while *Ghost* itself becomes a vanished breed of Hollywood film (evocative of its own fog-enshrouded fade-out), it continues to disclose cathartic contents in meaning relevant to gay men: as our community matures, many feel it is beneficial to discard aspects of our culture which allow for the continued perception that we are still immature as a group. Often this means the irreverent become irrelevant to the cause of appearing more serious (that is, older) to outsiders. But a very adult-minded *Ghost* quietly reveals that the realm of young-at-heart fantasy is not the domain of the childish. So a community espousing openness and acceptance should never close its doors to anyone no matter how childlike they act or appear. The gay moral of *Ghost*: we men must grow up, but we don't have to grow old in spirit.

Mrs. Muir's *fantasy companions:*
Ghostly movies have their place, but when it comes to film-y forces gay men seem to prefer the haunting (or humorous) to the more horrible types of spirited stories. Here are five examples and why:

★

The Bishop's Wife (1947)
Cary Grant as the most appealing angel, ever

Ghost (1990)
Whoopi Goldberg (and a shirtless Tony Goldwyn!)

Harvey (1950)
You can't see him but it doesn't mean he isn't there

Portrait of Jennie (1947)
The photography alone is from another dimension

The Uninvited (1944)
Spooky? Yes, but sweetly covered by the scent of mimosa

"I'm thinking how lonely she must have felt with her clean carpets."

Above: Spoken poignantly by Lucy Muir (Gene Tierney) to her "spirited" visitor, Captain Daniel Gregg (Rex Harrison), as he tells his life's story. *Left:* Lucy meets her ghostly cohabitator by candlelight for the first time. Kobal

The Heiress

1949. Paramount (AAN). Directed by William Wyler (AAN). Starring Olivia de Havilland (AA), Ralph Richardson (AAN), Montgomery Clift, Miriam Hopkins, Vanessa Brown, Betty Linley, Ray Collins, and Mona Freeman.

★

The basic story: A plain-faced and shy-mannered heiress falls quickly and deeply in love with a dashingly handsome and charming suitor, whom her arrogant father believes is only interested in marriage for money.

★

While writing his classic novel *Washington Square* (upon which *Heiress* is based), was it Henry James's sole intention—an author whom many say was blessed with a gift for bringing to full flower his female protagonists—to illustrate four personality traits (shy, silly, slick, and strict) that can be found in a single woman with his four lead players? Or was the quartet the scribe's own conscious (or unconscious) exposure of what he—a gentleman often rumored to be gay—found within himself?

No doubt straight audiences watching *Heiress* will come to their own conclusions. However, it is a safe bet that the gay viewer will find the four characters so recognizable as to be almost classic definitions taken from textbooks describing members of our own community, and will side with the latter theory. But the gay success of this parlor piece should also come as no surprise when you realize that each one of the actors playing these roles enjoyed great favor among our audience, and if any were to have been replaced by one less anointed the result would be less memorable.

"With one exception, my dear, you embroider . . . neatly."

Above: Spoken with disdain by Dr. Austin Sloper (Ralph Richardson) to his daughter, Catherine (Olivia de Havilland). *Right:* An *Heiress* publicity shot of Montgomery Clift (Morris Townsend) and Olivia de Havilland. Everett

Miriam Hopkins as *bubbly* Aunt Livinia:

After years of playing lead roles (and not always heroines) with a decidedly witchy edge, the time had come for Hopkins to move on to the character parts relegated to thespians of a certain age. Her befuddled but bemusing aunt reminds one of the party invitee who guarantees that the mood will be a festive one.

Olivia de Havilland as *benign* Catherine Sloper:

While she is rarely mentioned in the same breath as Davis and Crawford, de Havilland is assuredly one of the gay film fan's favorite actresses (and should be if she is not). Here she represents—in smashing, award-winning form—the meek and mild among us who lie in wait until the time comes for them to be their own person.

Ralph Richardson as *bitter* Dr. Austin Sloper:

One of the profession's greatest actors (English naturally), Richardson's unkind father is wholly unsympathetic but undeniably characteristic of those within our ranks who aspire to be "holier than thou"—and unarguably one of the best gay-ish male character roles on film.

Montgomery Clift as *beautiful* Morris Townsend:

Bar none, Clift was the screen's most important gay actor. It is just regrettable that he lived in a time when whispers of homosexuality could bring a career tumbling down (which in many ways is precisely what befell Clift). Like any gay man too pretty for words, the life of his Morris is led by looks. But is he mercenary as accused, or are we all, including the man himself, at the mercy of his appearance just to the point where our judgement is impaired?

2002. Miramax (AAN). Directed by Steve Daldry (AAN). Starring Nicole Kidman (AA), Meryl Streep, Julianne Moore (AAN), Ed Harris (AAN), Toni Collette, Jeff Daniels, Stephan Dillane, Miranda Richardson, John C. Reilly, Claire Danes, Allison Janney, and Jack Rovello.

★

The basic story: The lives of three women from three different periods are spiritually intertwined.

★

Before beginning our review, *Fabulous!* asks that readers give a moment of their time for thoughtful reflection—and good reason.

★

The triumphant end to World War II brought about the closing of another chapter in American history, less noted but no less impactful and far less celebrated by those most affected: women. To honor and reestablish soldiers, ladies who had so ably filled men's jobs during the conflict stepped aside, allowing them to resume their "rightful" places. This revisionism reclaimed every industry that had used the feminine in the face of a masculine void, and no business was as visibly changed as the movies.

Tinseltown literally and figuratively took the tailored suits off their actresses and placed them back on the shoulders of returning actors. And in that simple and unsuited gesture the golden age of the "women's picture" was stripped bare. While the gender changeover in cinematic content did not happen overnight—*femmes* held on to the *fatale* forties' end—by the start of the Eisenhower era women in pictures were fully redressed as mistresses tightly strapped to straight men's fantasies.

Unfortunately, Hollywood sees fit to re-dress this matter only sporadically. But as the genre's greatest (other than genuine female) followers, gay men mark the passage of time with prime examples—ranging wildly from Sally Field's *Norma Rae* to Toni Collette's *Muriel's Wedding*—until the dames get their ultimate due, and one of these moments surely came with the timely appearance of *The Hours*.

For those awaiting this genre's return in the dawning century, imagine the reaction to one example which held in store three epic epicene roles, and double that amount in excellent supporting feminine (and masculine) parts. But *Hours* was not watchable because its cast was heavily distaff; its minutes were memorable because they evoked the category's early days while provoking with a timely twist. Though the "provocative" is actually quite a subtle presence, the fact that the titled triad in *Hours* are "out" lesbians (or have tendencies) shows how far the "woman's picture" has come from being almost always about independent females who still depended on males being in or coming back to their lives.

But *Hours* also shows how far we gay males and the movies still have to go. While appreciating our "sisters" fine showing—and including Ed Harris's acclaimed role as a writer dying of AIDS—gay men have yet to see themselves in a showcase of equal content, stature, and praise. Obviously too many in Hollywood still fear that the sight of as many men in same-sex relationships would stop the clock cold. However, we will keep counting the hours until that deserved day comes.

" . . . you cannot find peace by avoiding life."

Above: Spoken by Virginia Woolf (Nicole Kidman) on a train platform, in a pleading conversation with her husband, Leonard Woolf (Stephan Dillane). *Left:* Virginia spending time peacefully in the grass with her niece Angelica Bell (Sophie Wyburd). Kobal

How to Marry a Millionaire

1953. Twentieth Century-Fox. Directed by Jean Negulesco. Starring Lauren Bacall, Marilyn Monroe, Betty Grable, William Powell, Cameron Mitchell, David Wayne, Rory Calhoun, Alexander D'Arcy, and Fred Clark.

★

The basic story: A trio of beautiful single women rent a large, expensive Manhattan apartment as a ruse for catching rich husbands.

★

To readers unfamiliar with the means and ways of gay men, it might be a good idea for *Fabulous!* to duly note—before writing about the "proposals" in *Marry*—that in same-sex relationships quite often one partner assumes society's historic "feminine" role in the partnership. Label if you must, but the point being made is that while some (straight men mainly) see the world in precise sexual terms of gender-based duties (breadwinners and bread bakers) gay men are not and cannot be so rigid in their domestic setups. Furthermore, gay men do not consider the idea of one man taking care of the other *financially* to be foreign or repellant. Thus, it should be comprehensible that when gay men watch a picture about ladies searching about for gentlemen with gobs of money, such as in *Marry*, we do not view the intentions of the female characters derogatorily as "gold-digging" so much as we, being able to see ourselves in their position, understand that "going for the gold" is not such a disrespectful way to go.

But a more interesting (and timely) turn has occurred in relation to the petticoated pursuers in *Marry*. Greater numbers of straight men now see the pursuit in this film as not such a bad idea after all, and don't mind the notion of themselves staying at home and letting their wives do the work. While on the other hand, more women find the manipulation in *Millionaire* an unwelcome reminder of the once-preferred subservience and suspicious motivations expected from their gender.

Fortunately, no current socio-sexual objections stop gay men from enjoying this film full of fortune hunters, frilly things, and enough members of either sex to let us pick and choose whom we most resemble: could it be Bacall (Schatze), Grable (Lola) or Monroe (Pola)? (each is *so* familiar that at times the film feels like a drag revue!); or most desire: again, even the men are so like the "boys." (But remember there are "daddies" and then there are guys who are just plain old! Rory Calhoun is a total hunk, but who would want to wed Fred Clark?)

A Marry *companion:*
Gentlemen Prefer Blondes is this film's obvious mate. But many readers may question why it is not one of the *Fabulous!* seventy-five. The answer helps shed a little light on the philosophy behind making these selections. Both are gay-fave movies, but *Gentlemen*, with its story of two showgirls loose on an ocean liner and in "gay" Paree, is not as easily relatable to us as is the basic mate-searching quest of the lovely trio in *Marry*. However, *Gentlemen* does contain two musical numbers so "gay" they are practically cultural cornerstones—Monroe's signature "Diamonds Are A Girl's Best Friend" and Russell's homoerotic "Ain't There Anyone Here for Love?" (where she is joined by a group of *dancing* male "athletes" obviously dressed to appear nearly naked!)—making it still highly recommended queer viewing.

"Look at Roosevelt, look at Churchill, look at old fella 'what's-his-name' in The African Queen.*"*

Above: Spoken by Schatze Page (Lauren Bacall) as justification for husband-hunting for a rich, older man (and as a Hollywood insider reference). *Right:* The three *Marry* roommates on their swanky Manhattan apartment terrace; from left, Pola Debovoise (Marilyn Monroe), Loco Dempsey (Betty Grable), and Schatze. Kobal

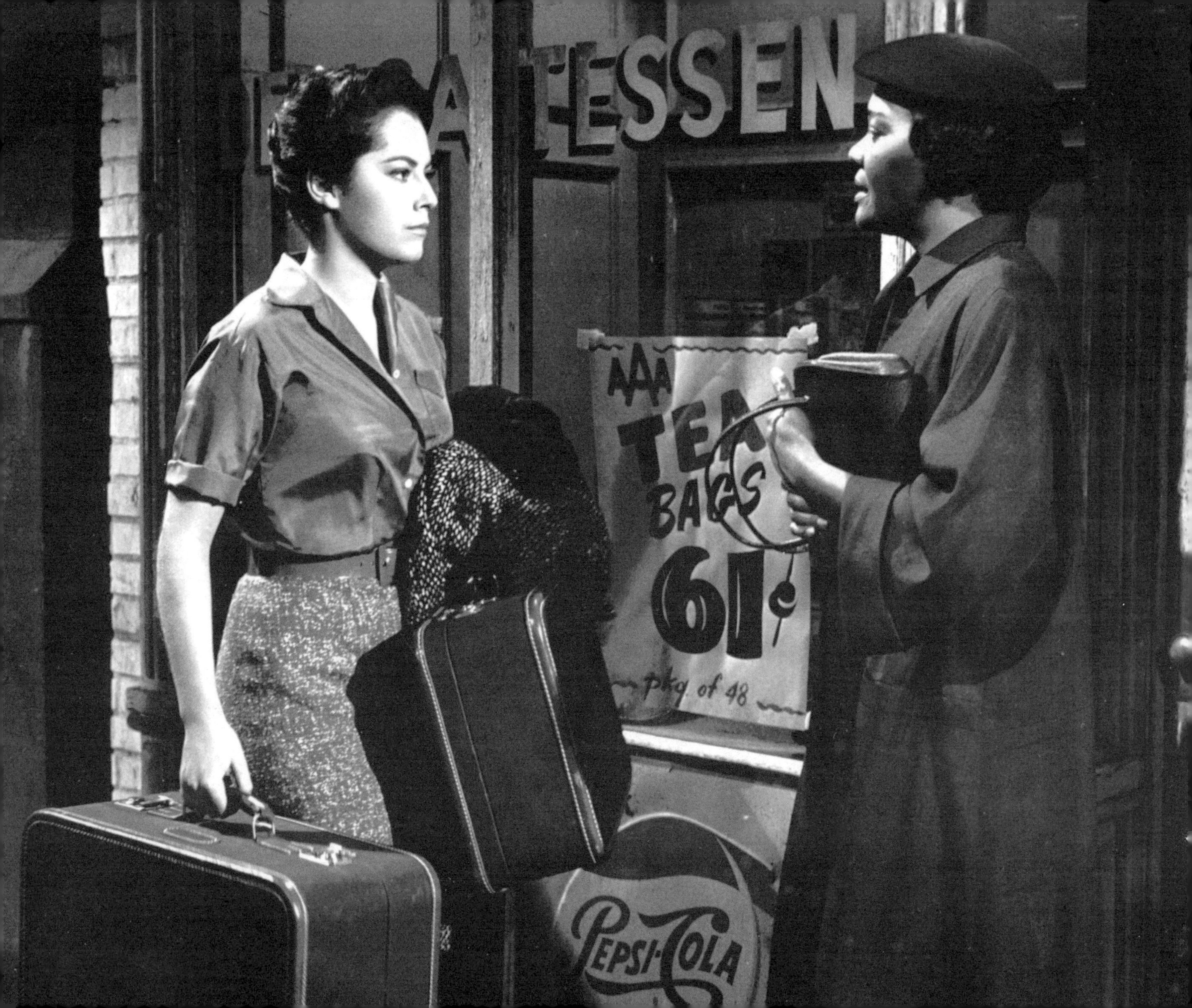
ESSEN
AAA
TEA
BAGS
61¢
pkg of 48
PEPSI-COLA

1959. Universal-International. Directed by Douglas Sirk. Starring Lana Turner, John Gavin, Juanita Moore (AAN), Susan Kohner (AAN), Sandra Dee, Dan O'Herlihy, Robert Alda, and Troy Donahue.

★

The basic story: A struggling white actress and her daughter befriend a homeless black mother and her little girl and offer to share their small apartment for the evening. But the short stay becomes a lifetime relationship, and as wealth replaces poverty, both mothers discover that their own aspirations and beliefs are not shared by their daughters.

★

For fans of thought simply presented, this over-the-top piece of cinema more than likely will not please (although its messages are no less noteworthy). However, to those who like their medicine given with a spoonful of sugar, tasting both sweet and tart, this large helping of melodramatics is sure to find a hungry audience. Notably, back in the not-so-*out*-there fifties, ladling with such a heavy hand was hardly out of the norm. It served as camouflage, allowing the really important stuff to be brought in like an apple in the puss of a garnished porcine platter. Yum. While this seems excessive, it was a necessary means if you wanted to convey anything meaningful—back when people were more closemouthed than open-minded.

However, few went as colorfully overboard when fudging the dark underbelly of their stories or were as good at glossing over their characters' flaws as director Douglas Sirk, a storyteller who was both superbly subversive and often far-too-flashy. But while others were afraid to even make a slight attempt, Sirk prettily pushed the cultural agenda in an era when pushing was often met with a hard shove back. Is it a wonder then why Sirk and his work are simultaneously revered and reviled by gay moviegoers? Gentlemen, please!

Whether one is for or against him, *Imitation* stands as his most gay-iconic movie. Few films have been able to mix such a spicy blend of classism, sexism, and racism into one bursting pie, richly smothered over with motherly love, that it makes you want to weep (which it does, often). Surely the cast—from ripe Turner to morsel Dee, too-*too* much Kohner and not enough Moore (with the cherry on top of Mahalia Jackson singing!)—could have enjoyed it, too, had they not been full from hamming it up or chewing the scenery. But for gay men especially it is the sentiment of "love who you are" that makes this film Sirk's most appealing meal. Enjoy the feast, men!

Imitation *at its most genuine:*
Gay men are suckers for showy starts, plus they help set the right mood, and the dazzling dropping diamond titles of *Life* are what grab us first. Here are five more with great beginnings:

★

Barbarella (1968) by Maurice Binder
Catch Me If You Can (2002) by Agnes Deygas
The Parent Trap (1961) by Xavier Atencio
The Pink Panther (1964) by DePatie-Freleng
Walk on the Wild Side (1962) by Saul Bass

"Eh, Miss Lora, you never asked."

Above: Spoken pointedly by "colored" housekeeper Annie Johnson (Juanita Moore) to her employer-friend Lora Meredith (Lana Turner) after the latter confesses to not knowing the former had any other friends. *Left:* Annie confronts her wayward, "light-skinned" daughter, Sarah Jane (Susan Kohner). Everett

L.A. Confidential

1997. Warner Bros. (AAN). Directed by Curtis Hanson (AAN). Starring Russell Crowe, Guy Pearce, Kevin Spacey, James Cromwell, Kim Basinger (AA), David Straithairn, Danny DeVito, Ron Rifkin, Matt McCoy, and Simon Baker.

★

The basic story: Two cops of differing temperaments trying to solve the same murder case discover guilt and corruption in a most shocking place.

★

Films appearing as glaringly heterosexual as *Confidential* seem out of place in the pages of a book with a focus on and about the homosexual film fan. Evidently, the *mucho machismo* in them is too much the antithesis of our kind's expected gentle ways. However, concluding that this film is "straight as an arrow" would be the summation of someone with "blinders on" or the conclusion drawn by the "uninformed eye." In any case, the not-so-clever deduction made by someone new to the ranks of astute cinephiles. For anyone who had been around some time would have arrived at a shockingly different position. Speaking most confidentially (as the "big bosses" wouldn't like this stuff to get out and blow the industry's cover), they would secretly pick this flick to be a surefire (in the libelous language of the scandal sheets it re-creates) "pansy pleaser."

While this overwhelming acceptance by an often underappreciated group may hardly have been an outward intention of *Confidential*, it is something producers must have seen inside its seamy scenario laden with far-from-hidden gay attractions: for-hire starlets made over as superstars, Simon Baker (from TV's *The Guardian*) as a beefy actor who would bed anyone for a chance at stardom, homo-twists (the queer-baiting of suspects), and, most gaily impassioned, the tantalizing turns between the pair of gorgeous male leads.

Yes, the "reel deal" for gay fans comes with the homosexually explosive relationship begging to burst out, involving "Mr. Good Cop" and "Mr. Not-So-Bad Cop" or, if you prefer, "Pretty Boy vs Hunky Daddy." As the "men in blue" buffly embodied by, respectively, Guy Pearce and Russell Crowe, the thought "What were the producers thinking?" pops out to be analyzed. But regardless of anything intended or happily accidental, by the time this film went into production, both men were already quite the rage in a community quick to spot "hot and hunky" talent. Notably, Pearce had just played, in pectorially perfect fashion, the role of Felicia Jollygoodfellow in *The Adventures of Priscilla, Queen of the Desert*, and Crowe came "out" to us as the gay son Jeff Mitchell in his *The Sum of Us.* Incidentally, both were 1994 Aussie indies. You gotta love those men down under!

★

Confidential *thought:*
Despite knowing it may lead to blows, what angry, envious, jealous, or unrequited message(s of love) is Pearce (Det. Exley) hoping to send out to Crowe (Officer White), whom his actions will clearly enflame, when he seduces but is not actually shown in bed with the hot-under-the-collar officer's new girlfriend, Lynn Bracken (played with Oscar-winning style by Kim Basinger)?

"A hooker cut to look like Lana Turner is still a hooker."

Above: Spoken too cockily by Det. Lt. Exley (Guy Pearce) to a woman he assumes is impersonating actress Lana Turner (Brenda Bakke) in Hollywood's Formosa restaurant. *Right:* Prostitute Lynn Bracken (Kim Basinger) and Det. Exley share an intimate moment. Kobal

1944. Twentieth Century-Fox. Directed by Otto Preminger (AAN). Starring Dana Andrews, Clifton Webb (AAN), Gene Tierney, Judith Anderson, Vincent Price, and Dorothy Adams.

★

The basic story: A detective investigating the murder of a young woman alters his methods when the deceased turns up alive. However, with a quite dead body still on his hands, his search continues for the perpetrator, while he falls for the original victim.

★

Nothing brings more confusion to gay men than a film which is softly made by the hands of a perceived moviemaking "heavy." It is something that makes no logical sense to those who firmly believe we are the sole possessors of the light cinematic touch. Fortunately, the instances when our sensibility can be produced by someone outside the confines of the community is rare—and barely do they glitter. Yet it is because of the uniqueness of the occurence when straight men meddle successfully in queer film areas that *Laura* stands as a golden beacon, and if there is any shadow cast across this noir classic it is cast by the man who is responsible for its resplendence, famed director Otto Preminger.

For a man who came to be as well known for womanizing (his alleged affairs with actresses Jean Seberg and Dorothy Dandridge come to mind) as filmmaking, the, shall we say, "womanliness" of *Laura* is astonishing. True, the film has manly moments: as when studly cop Mark McPherson, played by studly Dana Andrews, can hardly hold back his homophobic distaste of the dandies

dribbling about; and when the romance between Andrews and Tierney feels almost forcefully inserted. But these heterosexual interludes do not lie at the "gay" heart of *Laura.* Actually, it is queerness of every shape and form which does, and this includes everything from the pithy-lined screenplay, the twisted plot, the too-devoted housekeeper (Dorothy Adams), and the too-fey-to-fight suitor (Vincent Price, playing a male gigolo who is being kept by, of all the women in the world, Judith Anderson!), to the famous Raksin score poured over the top of the proceedings like cologne in a gay bar.

But, really, what about *Laura* is the queerest thing of them all? Well, *Fabulous!* would have to answer that question with the name, unhesitatingly, of actor Clifton Webb, who played mincing mentor Waldo Leyendecker to Gene Tierney's glam girl on the career rise. Webb became the "next big thing" thanks to his preening in a picture already densely populated by strutting peacocks and was something quite noteworthy because he kept his homosexuality not much of a secret in Hollywood. But it's a more significant sign of the times that Preminger went out on a limb when casting a reedy unknown in this important implied heterosexual role in the first place. Maybe Otto ain't so "heavy" after all.

Here are five more films with men in "soft" support:

★

James Coco in *Only When I Laugh* (1981)
John Gielgud in *Arthur* (1981)
Daniel Massey in *Star!* (1968)
Robert Preston in *Victor/Victoria* (1982)
Russ Tamblyn in *Peyton Place* (1957)

"I can afford a blemish on my character, but not on my clothes."

Above: Spoken by cowardly kept man Shelby Carpenter (Vincent Price) to Det. Lt. Mark McPherson (Dana Andrews). *Left:* Det. McPherson questions victim-turned-suspect Laura (Gene Tierney). Kobal

Law of Desire (La Ley del Deseo)

1987. El Deseo (Spain). Directed by Pedro Almodovar. Starring Eusebio Poncela, Carmen Maura, Antonio Banderas, Miguel Molina, Fernando Guillén, Manuela Velasco, Nacho Martinez, and Bibi Andersen.

★

The basic story: A writer-director loves one man unrequitedly, but is in a relationship with another whose jealousy leads to murder, loss, and redemption.

★

When is a "gay" film not gay? The answer: a film is *not* "gay" if it is seen first as "foreign" (even if it is still full of men-loving men). But before going further with this "foreign vs gay" discussion, it is necessary that readers go back a few years in their minds—to the mid-late eighties—because the timing of *Law* is of the essence.

Back in the days of Boy George and the first President George Bush, films from faraway places were most often shown in theaters called "art film" houses. (These places still exist today, of course, but in fewer numbers.) While movies played inside these cramped spaces did not always earn the "creative" title, the protective environment gave these pictures a wide berth to show adults *unadulterated* content (and this gave the theater itself merit). Foreign filmmakers, many of whom did not have to contend with the same levels of domestic censorship, took advantage of this situation and stuffed their films full of scintillating subject matter. Having always looked somewhat more open-mindedly upon sexuality, too, auteurs abroad were less concerned with labels, "gay" or otherwise. Consequently, when their wares ran our way, they easily overflowed with scenes many saw as questionable, inappropriate, or just plain pornographic, and such was the look of *Desire* when it first appeared Stateside.

Those expecting a simple Spanish "dish" were served something almost "too hot to handle" when director Pedro Almodovar (who went on to become the most-praised openly gay director in cinema) pulled out all the stops in his mixed bag of the fast, furious, and transgendered females. However, no one in the film shot to fame as quickly as Antonio Banderas, who became an instant gay icon when he topped-off his star-making appearance by being "topped" by a man for all the cultured world to see (which amazingly seemed not to lessen his hetero-dream lover status, too). This was definitely *nothing* you were going to see in an American film (come to think of it, we ain't seen nothin' like it yet!), and brings up a timely thought: If *Law* were shown today, would fewer straight people end up seeing its upended star because films are now being marketed even more to specific audience members? Possibly. Many new doors have opened recently, but many older ones, which allowed those to *mistakenly* wander in, may have closed.

Five more fine foreigners whose films we've fancied:

★

Javier Bardem

Alain Delon

Jean Marais

Olivier Martinez

Marcello Mastroainni

"¿Tú quieres chingarme, verdád?" ("You want to screw me, don't you?")

Above: Spoken wantonly by Antonio (Antonio Banderas) to the man he is obsessed with, director Pablo Quintero (Eusebio Poncela), the first time they are in bed together. *Right:* Scene still of Antonio in his lover's apartment. Everett

1975. Paramount. Directed by Berry Gordy. Starring Diana Ross, Billy Dee Williams, Anthony Perkins, Jean-Pierre Aumont, Nina Foch, Beau Richards, and Marisa Mell.

★

The basic story: An attractive woman from the ghetto dreams of becoming a world-famous fashion designer. But to realize her ambitions she must make personal sacrifices to those not interested in her talent, and upon reaching her goal, she sees hers as a hollow victory.

★

While at the risk of having it sound like a massive overstatement, *Fabulous!* is going to say that *Mahogany* occupies a more special spot in gay favorite moviedom than most other films herein. Whoa! However, to fully grasp this implausible concept one must look at the film—which *Fabulous!* does not consider a great piece of "gay" cinema even though it is a fashionable, *color*-updated "woman's picture"—in context with its mid-seventies setting.

The year 1975, if you are old enough to remember, was a time when disco was king, and queens were just then coming into their own as straight people began accepting our existence, which heretofore had been, in the earlier pre-Stonewall years, considered virtually zero. (To gay men used to being out in the open and part of everyday life, think what this must have been like.)

But even while mainstream was just getting used to seeing gay men "in the flesh," they had long seen one of our culture's most sublimely tangible creations, the "diva" (an important woman to us because she acted as surrogate in our relationships with men—in a world which *still* does not love the idea). However, even the

divas themselves were seen by many as "old guard" in this new fairyland. So, to the names Bette, Joan, Judy, and others, was added Bette (Midler), Cher, Barbra, Liza, and, most definitely, Diana.

While all of these women actively served as role models for their own sex, races, and for others as well, the divine Miss Ross was a standout to the young gay community because our admiration for her threw us into a mix—which we shall slyly place into a chest made out of *Mahogany*—already full of people that had trouble fitting in with themselves without the "boys" being added. Imagine then, if you can, what it was like having all these individuals (blacks, whites, straights, gays, men, women, and more) dropped for the first time into this one spot (a theater) in 1975, and you should be able to puzzle out why it is that a badly made *Mahogany* box (filled with the cheesiest stuff) sits in such a "fab" spot.

★

The "gayest" things kept inside Mahogany:
• a fashion spectacle *designed* by none other than Miss Ross herself (and it shows!)
• a fashion montage (oh, how we love 'em)
• a "gun scene," way too phallicly handled by Billy Dee Williams (as boyfriend Brian) and Anthony Perkins (as closeted photographer Sean)
• a lesbian-ish owner of a fragrance factory, Carlotta Gavina (Marisa Mell)
• a "bitchy" fashion designer (played in a bit part by our very own Bruce Vilanch!)
• a huge hit theme song: "Do You Know Where You're Going To"
• a hot-wax-dripping-candle party scene!

"Success is nothing without someone you love to share it with."

Above: Spoken by Brian (Billy Dee Williams) to his girlfriend Tracy (Diana Ross) after she has become a sensation as model Mahogany. *Left:* Mahogany modeling one of her own creations, to negative response, in a charity fashion show. Kobal

Mildred Pierce

"With this money, I can get away from you. From your chickens and your pies and your kitchens and everything that smells of grease."

1945. Warner Bros. (AAN). Directed by Michael Curtiz. Starring Joan Crawford (AA), Ann Blyth (AAN), Eve Arden (AAN), Jack Carson, Bruce Bennett, Zachary Scott, Lee Patrick, and Butterfly McQueen.

★

The basic story: A slavish mother of two girls separates from her husband and works first as a waitress, then as a restaurateur to support her family. However, her professional triumphs are undermined by personal adversity.

★

This far-from-black film noir has so much going for it that gay men have no trouble expressing their undivided love. Actually, *Mildred* has everything a gay film fan could want from a "dame" (and that ain't no small feat): a great director (Michael Curtiz); a crackerjack script filled with priceless Oscar-nominated Ranald MacDougall lines ("I made tips, and was glad to get them") based on a story by James Cain, author of *The Postman Always Rings Twice*; beautiful shots (via Ernest Haller's framing shadows, AAN); delightfully dated costumes (the hats alone make *Mildred* a must-see queer event); a moody musical score (courtesy of composer Max Steiner); one "swell" (buff Bruce Bennett, onetime movie Tarzan, as Bert Pierce); one "slicker" (fox-faced Zachary Scott, as wily Monte Beragon); and last, but by no means least, ace acting dealt by three leading ladies.

Between Crawford, Blyth, and Arden, it is hard to decide who deserves the most gay attention. As fans of the real-life Mommie Dearest know, Crawford's titular role was the actress's effort at redemption to those calling her box-office "bad news." Her matron of dishonor was an Oscar-winning tour-de-force performance to be reckoned with and one that returned Joan to her rightful place. Blyth was a newcomer to film, but she shows no frosh jitters in her fresh-mouthed portrayal of the daughter from hell, Veda. (The fact that in later years Blyth sold cupcakes to kids as a bakery spokesperson is truly twisted.) Then there is Arden, an actress fast being forgotten by film audiences, straight *and* gay, but whose work in *Pierce* (as the cracking-wise Ida) should restore an unforgettable impression of her supporting acting roles that were far from secondary contributions.

★

What "hurts" in Pierce:
After about twenty minutes, Butterfly McQueen (as the maid Lottie) flutters into *Mildred*, and her dizzy black helper is a spin back to when movies were color-blind.

Mildred's nasty relations:
Veda Pierce is too venomous for some, but Ann Blyth's role falls into one of our favorite film categories: the "bitch." Here is a further quintet of "pissed-off" performances to watch—from a safe distance:

★

Judith Anderson as Mrs. Danvers
in *Rebecca* (1940)

Anne Bancroft as Mrs. Robinson
in *The Graduate* (1967)

Louise Fletcher as Nurse Ratchett
in *One Flew Over the Cuckoo's Nest* (1975)

Angela Lansbury as Mrs. Iselin
in *The Manchurian Candidate* (1962)

Barbara O'Neil as Duchess de Praslin
in *All This and Heaven Too* (1940)

1981. Paramount. Directed by Frank Perry. Starring Faye Dunaway, Diana Scarwid, Steve Forrest, Howard da Silva, Mara Hobel, Rutanya Alda, Harry Goz, Michael Edwards, Jocelyn Brando, and Priscilla Pointer.

★

The basic story: A biopic of the great Hollywood star Joan Crawford, as seen through the eyes of her adopted and allegedly abused daughter, Christina.

★

To have this Mommie following another (Mildred Pierce) is not just coincidence, it helps *Fabulous!* move the editorial along by bringing up some points about gay men and their movie likes which would be much harder to do if either summary was located pages away. Lucky you!

Both of these films are essentially, but abstractly, about the same person: Joan Crawford. Yet each represents the star in a different light: the first quite good, the second very bad. Joan in *Mildred* is a showpiece of the actress's work (and one hopes of the actress herself) at the highest level. *Pierce* is a devoted, selfless, strong survivor whom anyone would place upon a pedestal (and naturally gay men constructed one for her). However, *Mommie* shows Joan (in the ludicrously lurid face of Faye Dunaway) as the lowest type of woman imaginable: selfish, manipulative, abusive, you name it, and not a person anyone would want to place on high. Strangely enough, gay men still took to her like the devil's minions.

What this twisted affection to two different sides of the same person says about us as a group brings us to one of those points about gay men: Do we dote on gossip? (Readers, don't bother to answer, this is a hypothetical *Fabulous!* question.) For if we are too fond of chatter, to whom else could a film full of the rants and raves of a clearly partial voice (Christina Crawford's) be intended? And to whom else did producers think this peeling away of the glamorous façade of a famed movie queen would appeal? Likely a group fascinated with fallacy, because deep down we believe that almost everybody, including ourselves, is a little phony. Baloney, you say? Maybe. But while *Fabulous!* feels that the campy carnage of this film may be the hook, it still does not render false the point that *Mommie* is solely about skewering someone whom we once worshipped and were responsible, at least partially, for making into an icon—and that we choose *not* to look away. Instead we watch *Dearest* leeringly and guiltily, like it was a filmed car wreck.

Fabulous! apologizes for the downbeat tone to those who were expecting something of an upbeat review. However, if readers can get clear that our connection to Crawford's crash herein is at least a big part of the *Dearest* attraction, we can go on to superficially fun reasons for why we watch this Halloween masquerade ball—like the whacked-out scene when Crawford assumes her ill daughter's role in the soap opera *Secret Storm*, even though the part was for a thirty year old and Joan was past sixty! But like the wheel-within-a-wheel enigma, this is still skin-deep attraction to a shallow moment in a film that is built on spinning tales not totally proven true *or* false, and the circle will keep going around and around unless you choose to look deeper into the darkness that lies at the heart of this *Dearest* of gay movie favorites.

"Helga, I'm not mad at you, I'm mad at the dirt!"

Above: Spoken too enthusiastically by Joan Crawford (Faye Dunaway) to one of her servants while they clean the floor together. *Left:* Adopted Christina Crawford (Mara Hobel) cutting her birthday cake with her charitable mother. Kobal

1987. MGM (AAN). Directed by Norman Jewison (AAN). Starring Cher (AA), Nicholas Cage, Vincent Gardenia (AAN), Olympia Dukakis (AA), Danny Aiello, John Mahoney, and Anita Gillette.

★

The basic story: A lonely Italian bookkeeper gets engaged, but while her intended is away unwittingly falls in love with his brother.

★

Gay men have scores of favorite film stars filling the heavens. But what turns one of these bright luminaries into a "superstar" who leaves the others behind in the cosmic dust? Is it stellar talents, beauty, intelligence, humor, *and* the ability to survive over infinite periods of time? Hmmm. Does this dazzling description already sound to you like someone fabulously familiar? Could it be describing—*uhmmm*—Cher? Yes, you clever readers, you are indeed correct. *Fabulous!* is speaking of the "eternal one," to whom the depiction fits like a beaded, barely-there Bob Mackie gown. And speaking of eternities, just how long has it been since gay men wholeheartedly fell for this sexy sylph?

It is precisely our lengthy and undisputable devotion to Cher which explains why *Moonstruck* is a part of *Fabulous!* The film may stand on its own as an excellent entry into the romantic-comedy genre, deservedly praised and financially rewarded, but had it not been for the personage of our dear "dark lady," *Moonstruck* would likely have been struck out of consideration. Without Cher this is a great but not gaily made film. With her, *Moonstruck* automatically came across our gaydar so that we could quickly determine if the film was an unfriendly threat,

UFO (unidentifiable as a favorable object), or something heading happily toward our home base (which this one then ended up doing). Bear in mind, automatic "gay" tracking can mete out strategic miscalculations. Often if a force is seen as most friendly, as is Cher, the results can be the watching of the unwatchable (see below).

But *Fabulous!* digresses. Time to climb back on to the good ship *Moonstruck*, which in addition to the commanding gay lead of captain Cher has other persons on board quite capable of steering things our way. Olympia Dukakis struck gold—with us and with Oscar—for her performance, and continued doing so as the transsexual Mrs. Anna Madrigal (in Armistead Maupin's *Tales of the City*). Another fully able-bodied individual is male lead Nicholas Cage, who struck many at the time as a quirky (queer) choice for leading man. However, gentlemen who fall into the slightly off-center personality category often head to the top of the gay man's list of most attractive actors. And many of the boys would have given their right hand (get it?!) for an opportunity to tame Cage's unkempt, caged-animal character.

Cher's gayest?:

Though short on selections, our attraction to this captivating creature's film output is a full 99 percent (the 1 percent outstanding, 1996's *Faithful*). But of the rest, perhaps the one that hits us closest is *Mask* (1985). As the story of a mother who loves her deformed (misfit) son unconditionally, it fully embodies what we expect this woman feels toward everyone in our community. The only reason why it may not have been picked as the Cher *Fabulous!* film choice was its too-somber tone.

"When you love them they drive you crazy because they know they can."

Above: Spoken advisingly by Rose Castorini (Olympia Dukakis) to her daughter Loretta Castorini (Cher) in a discussion of the latter's illicit romance. *Right:* Loretta and her controversial consort, Ronny Cammareri (Nicholas Cage), attend a night at the opera. Everett

Mr. Blandings Builds His Dream House

1948. RKO. Directed by H. C. Potter. Starring Cary Grant, Myrna Loy, Melvyn Douglas, Reginald Denny, Sharyn Moffett, Connie Marshall, Louise Beavers, Ian Wolfe, Harry Shannon, Nestor Paiva, Jason Robards, and Lex Barker.

★

The basic story: A married couple, tired of occupying a too-small inner-city apartment with their two daughters and a live-in maid, buys and moves into a larger country dwelling. Unfortunately, the property they select turns out to be much more trouble to get into shape than they had anticipated.

★

Filmmakers determine how all the many individual parts of a film are made so that when the pieces are put together a work of solid craftsmanship has (hopefully) been created. Now if producers want to soften the construction of their film a bit—making it easier for *sensitive* viewers to watch—two main things would need adjusting: "the premise(s) of the story" and "the performers in the piece." And just by chance, with this particular *Dream House*, you happened upon a film which does a queenly job of clarifying, thusly:

The Premise(s) of the Story

1. Homeownership. Some may think otherwise, but gay men, as much as straights, have the same desire of owning a home. Okay, maybe the vision doesn't include a white picket fence as much as a stunning city view, but the domestic wish is there regardless.

2. Consumerism. In a sly snipe at the "system," while "Mr." is in advertising and his job is getting people to buy stuff, both he and the "Missus" love spending money impulsively and indulgently on what they feel they deserve but can't really afford. (By the way, how does a family of four living on fifteen grand a year pay for a live-in maid?)

3. Decorating. Both have our sensibilities (most delightfully obvious in *Dream*'s gayest scene: Loy picking paint colors) and sense about how our soon-to-be showplace should look.

4. Modern relations. He is clearly the "worker bee" and she is unarguably the "queen," but they both banter and buzz equally around their hive.

The Performers in the Piece

1. Myrna Loy. Because her demeanor was never mean and her poise never misplaced, gay men are forever devoted to this fair beauty.

2. Cary Grant. One could assume that his alleged homosexuality is the reason why gay men are so attracted. But the truth is it matters not, for even if he were one of "them" we'd still be smitten by his sophisticated and sexy self. (*Fabulous!* does not know who to credit for bringing these two together—Loy and Grant—but it seems theirs was a match made just for us.)

3. Melvyn Douglas, Reginald Denny, and Lex Barker. For the ultimate consumers, *House* gives gay men plenty to shop for. But it is bit-playing *uber*-hunk Barker who is the biggest and best-looking bargain.

"If you ain't eatin' Wham, you ain't eatin' ham!"

Above: Spoken brightly by live-in housekeeper Gussie (Louise Beavers) to her employer, Jim Blandings (Cary Grant), who then uses it as the slogan for a client of his ad agency. *Left:* Muriel Blandings (Myrna Loy) and her husband go over architectural details with their designer, Henry Simms (Reginald Denny). Everett

Murder on the Orient Express

1974. EMI. Directed by Sidney Lumet. Starring Albert Finney (AAN), Ingrid Bergman (AA), Lauren Bacall, Sean Connery, Vanessa Redgrave, Richard Widmark, Michael York, John Gielgud, Anthony Perkins, Wendy Hiller, Jacqueline Bisset, Martin Balsam, Rachel Roberts, Jean-Pierre Cassel, Colin Blakely, George Coulouris, and Denis Quilley.

★

The basic story: A detective investigates a murder committed on board the luxury train on which he is originally just a passenger, and his suspects are his fellow travelers, a small select group of workers and the well-to-do.

★

Murder is something most foul, and the only way many gay men can deal with the vileness of such a crime is to look at it from a safe distance (in a cushy armchair is nice, maybe with a throw and a hot cup of cocoa) and hope that those being held for questioning are a glamorous, sophisticated, good-looking, and rich lot, or, at the very least, queerish oddballs. If that is the case, getting to the bottom of things before bedtime, along with whoever's in charge (hmmm, it looks like that could be the heavy, thick-accented man—Mr. Finney, presumably—who slathers on hand creams and trusses up his waxed mustache at night!), can be quite a bit of fun, without the worry of bodily harm. Unfortunately, if everything is not pleasing to the eyes and ears, or comfy-cozy, trying to find *whodunit* can be, well, just murder. (Note: *Fabulous!* believes "murder mysteries" are a gay favorite genre because they let us use our minds and not worry—gym bunnies aside—if we've got enough muscle.)

"There are too many clu-hoos in this ro-hoom!"

Above: Spoken by Inspector Poirot (Albert Finney), while investigating the murder scene, to Bianchi (Martin Balsam) and the Doctor (George Coulouris). *Right:* The Inspector, center, gives details of the crime to the assembled "star" suspects, including, from left to right, Jean-Pierre Cassel, Anthony Perkins, Vanessa Redgrave, Sean Connery, Ingrid Bergman, George Coulouris, Rachel Roberts, Wendy Hiller, Denis Quilley, Michael York, Jacqueline Bisset, Lauren Bacall, and Martin Balsam. Everett

It so happens that if you are in the mood to solve a deadly crime comfortably, and in style, *Express* is *the* way to go (and a gay old time the journey will be, too). Its cast of (then, in 1974) Hollywood's best and brightest talent resembles as much a caravan of the upper and lower classes as it does a seminar at the Actor's Studio. To those who love watching movie stars—and you know who you are—this is one you can't take your eyes off of (although turning down the sound is recommended when Bacall's on screen). What really makes *Orient* an opiate, though, is so many gay favorite actors in basically one room on wheels (yes, a tad close) and that each suspect seems so willing to throw themselves upon the mercy of our court—even a valiant and still very masculine Sean Connery. And since the only possible homophobe is the murder victim (Richard Widmark), what other conclusions could be drawn with Sir John Gielgud and Tony Perkins chief among those under suspicion?

Express companions:
Gathering many stars into a single film of any genre is one surefire way to attract a gay audience. Unfortunately, nowadays it is too costly doing so on a regular basis (as was not so much the case when *Orient* departed). While waiting for the next new densely actor-packed procession, why not watch one of these disparate five:

★

Around the World in Eighty Days (spectacle, 1956)
Earthquake (adventure, 1974)
Gosford Park (mystery, 2001)
Pepe (comedy, 1960)
Separate Tables (drama, 1958)

1964. Warner Bros. (AA). Directed by George Cukor (AA). Starring Rex Harrison (AA), Audrey Hepburn, Stanley Holloway (AAN), Wilfred Hyde-White, Gladys Cooper (AAN), Jeremy Brett, Theodore Bikel, Mona Washbourne, Isobel Elsom, and John Holland.

★

The basic story: A professor of languages wagers a visitor that within a few months he can transform a pupil—a poor Cockney flower girl—into a "lady" by teaching her poise and proper English.

★

Something queer happens when you bring up the subject of this film. You quickly find gay men are either solidly for or against it, with very few neutral votes. Considering how all-over-the-rainbow the film's proceedings are, *Fabulous!* would have to say this is a rare solidly divided reaction, and even more profound when you realize we were all on the same pro side in the beginning.

Way back when George Bernard Shaw published "Pygmalion"—his erudite essay on two "confirmed" bachelors endeavoring to make over a flower girl (hel-loo!)—gay men went ga-ga and stayed agog when the first film appeared: *Pygmalion* (1938), with Wendy Hiller as a perfect Eliza and Leslie Howard, the quintessential effete English actor, playing the prissy professor of elocution Henry Higgins. Sentiment changed (as did Shaw's own) only when the work became a musical. This was not opposition to setting things to music for the stage—how could it be?—but to "tampering with an original," a cardinal gay sin. But the deed was done. However, when *Pygmalion* premiered as such a great *Lady*, few found fault, and things were back on track.

Then the unthinkable happened. The hit staging brought heterosexuals into the fold in *very* large numbers. Suddenly, a classic for the gay ages was tainted with the supreme spoiler: straight fans. However, we held on knowing *we were there first* until the next revolution occurred: when Hollywood came a-courting, and the *Lady* was powerless to resist. Gay followers only hoped that she wouldn't be made over in the wrong way, as so many Broadway transfers had been mishandled in the past. However, we were emboldened to hear that Cukor would direct and Beaton would dress. How could we lose? But then the worst news arrived: Julie Andrews, the Great White Way's lead in *Lady* (and overnight sensation, thanks in part to our help) was passed over in favor of Audrey Hepburn. Though gay men never blamed Audrey (whose singing was *dubbed!!!!*), this offense of not hiring the original theater star to repeat her big role, combined with all the other infringements, forever stained the reputation of our once so fair *Lady*.

Now you have the story of why something so flowery (watch those opening credits, boys!) has lost its fragrant bloom for some. But *Fabulous!* wants to be fair about all this, and asks readers to take a look at this *luverly* film—with a most adorable Jeremy Brett as Freddy and a most queeny Rex Harrison as Professor Higgins (could any man act more prim on film and still try to pass himself off as straight?)—to see if it is a too-thorny rose to behold or simply "gay" as a daisy.

Lady's *girlfriend:*
Gigi (1958, AA), Lerner and Loewe's written-direct-for-the-screen musical, beautifully Beatonized and Minnelli-ed.

"Why can't a woman be more like a man?"

Above: Spoken by Professor Higgins (Rex Harrison) to Colonel Pickering (Wilfred Hyde-White). *Left:* Freddy Eynsforth-Hill (Jeremy Brett) beside a newly refined Eliza Doolittle (Audrey Hepburn), as she screams for horse Dover to move his "arse" at the Ascot, while Higgins looks on and Pickering looks away. Kobal

1959. MGM. Directed by Alfred Hitchcock. Starring Cary Grant, Eva Marie Saint, James Mason, Martin Landau, Leo G. Carroll, and Jesse Royce Landis.

★

The basic story: A rakish adman is mistaken for a spy by a debonair master criminal and his entourage. In his attempt to clear up the misunderstanding, the elegant exec is wrongly accused of committing murder. He flees to escape capture, while pursuing the true culprits.

★

In what direction, sexually, Hitchcock was taking *North* we may never truly know. But surely if this film were remade frame for frame today gay alarms would go off everywhere because they are literally flipped on from the very start (along with Saul Bass's urbane titles and Bernard Herrmann's near-best score) with this protracted misters-en-scène:

1. The attractive advertising executive tells his secretary to write down this thought for him to consider on the following day: "Think thin." (Ahem.)

2. The man proceeds to miscommunicate information about the "theater date" he is having with his mother (Jesse Royce Landis) and her friends later that night.

3. Over drinks with cronies at the Plaza, he attempts to call in and correct the error, but when exiting the bar is mistaken for a spy by a pair of bespoke baddies (one of whom clasps his cigarette quite *queerly*).

4. The duo then kidnap him to a Long Island manse, where he is questioned by another "suit" (James Mason) and his "catty" second-in-command (Martin Landau).

5. Unable to get what he wants, the "top man" departs with a nod to his well-heeled henchmen, with the expectation that they properly deal with things.

6. Instead of the usual fistfight, the tailored trio forceably plies the man with drink, whereupon the straight man's lament "Boy was I drunk last night" quickly comes to mind when last we see four good-looking grown men scuffling on the couch. (Another ahem, please.)

7. The now-soused hero is placed in a convertible, with the expectation that he will drive himself off a cliff.

8. Luckily, he lands not in the Sound but in jail, and is manhandled by a "daddy" cop with very hairy forearms and a most *queer*-sounding name, Emile Klinger.

★

With this as the opening inside his most stylish film, a clever story of false identities (racily written by Ernest Lehman) that turns as often as its notorious biplane, and the most phallic fade-out in movie history, maybe Hitchcock knew exactly where *North* was headed. But really the queerest sight in this film is more a subtle *bi*-lateral shift, which can barely be espied when the two most dastardly dandies move against each other while readying for a getaway. In their too-chic mountaintop hideaway, the head honcho (Mason) first calls his underling "touching" when the man (Landau) expresses concern over the motives of the boss's girlfriend (Saint). But then the senior sinister partner *too*-easily hurts his hand after punching junior when the subordinate further exposes his escort (can you say "beard"?), utilizing what the man himself calls his own "woman's intuition." Even if the "directions" are still vague, aside from the gay obviousness of *Strangers on a Train* and *Rope*, and the subtlety of *Rebecca*, *North* is the master's queerest, clearly.

"That's funny . . . the plane's dustin' crops where there ain't no crops."

Above: Spoken perplexedly by the bus-waiting man at Prairie Crossing (Malcolm Atterbury) to fugitive Roger O. Thornhill (Cary Grant). *Right:* Thornhill berates spy Eve Kendall (Eva Marie Saint) in front of her lover Phillip Vandamm (James Mason) inside a Chicago auction house. Everett

1942. Warner Bros. Directed by Irving Rapper. Starring Bette Davis (AAN), Claude Rains, Paul Henreid, Gladys Cooper (AAN), John Loder, Bonita Granville, Ilka Chase, Lee Patrick, Franklin Pangborn, and Mary Wickes.

★

The basic story: A spinster, suffering at the hands of an abusive mother, is committed to a sanatorium where she regains her health and independence. But upon her release she falls for an unhappily married man—with a troubled child of his own. Then, returning home, the daughter finds that her mother expects things to pick up where they were left off.

★

Ask any person who the top gay favorite female stars are and they—gay, straight, or from another planet—will answer, unhesitatingly, with these three names: Judy, Joan, and Bette. (For those who just rolled their eyes at this reply, *Fabulous!* asks that some respect be shown our old friends while awaiting the arrival of new ones—whom we all agree are needed.) But as unanimous a decision as it is naming the trio, trying to choose definitive films from careers full of choice work—and ones which have some meaning to gay culture—is a problem without any easy or absolute solutions.

However, the time is here for the best of Bette, and, after a journey of much deliberation, *Voyager* was found to be the one. The reasons why *Now* was chosen and others were not are simple (but may still not satisfy those upset by the choice). For example, had her performance in *All About Eve* not come after her "peak," *Fabulous!* would have been all about it, but it did; her sensational *Jezebel* was a Southern belle ringer, but the rest of the film didn't ring enough bells; and her unrepentant murderess in *The Letter* was a killer, but shot out no obvious queer signals.

And so across Davis's résumé *Fabulous!* searched until *Now*, and the voyage ended. No, *Now* does not show Bette at her most ruthless (see below), but it does do her up in ermine—which is often just as exquisite an experience. It also has a story line torn straight from the pages of any gay man's favorite novel: dowdy girl, beset upon by hellish mother, confesses to illicit past, smoking, and box-making to quaint and cuddly doctor who recommends spa treatment; woman reemerges—in open-toed sandals and picture hat (makeover!)—as the mysterious lady who delays day-trippers on a lavish South American cruise; has it out with miserable matriarch back home, in Back Bay Boston, causing latter's heart to stop beating; and becomes fairy godmother to misfit child of handsome lover. Even if it's not *Now*, it is still all this and gay heaven, too, in one movie. What more could any of you "little foxes" and "old acquaintances" hope for?

★

The "bons" in Voyager:
• Gladys Cooper, as the malevolent mom.
• Mary Wickes, as the snappy nurse.
• Franklin Pangborn, as the "cruise" director.
• Max Steiner, as the music maestro.
• Smoking, as in foreplay (cough!).

The "worst" side of Bette?:
Some may disagree, but *Fabulous!* feels the coldest Bette gets is her chilling performance in *Little Foxes* (1941), as Regina "the grits is cold" Giddens. Brrrr!

"Charlotte is no more ill than a molting canary."

Above: Spoken dismissively by Mrs. Henry Vale (Gladys Cooper) to Dr. Jaquith (Claude Rains) about the mental state of her daughter Charlotte Vale (Bette Davis). *Left:* Charlotte, with her soon-to-be lover Jerry Durrance (Paul Henried), is thinking about what her mother might be thinking at that same moment. Kobal

1966. Embassy. Directed by Russell Rouse. Starring Stephen Boyd, Elke Sommer, Tony Bennett, Eleanor Parker, Milton Berle, Joseph Cotten, Jill St. John, Edie Adams, Ernest Borgnine, and many more.

★

The basic story: A handsome heel of an actor has risen to the height of his profession, and has an Oscar nomination to show for his efforts. But while he prepares for the main event, an abused friend recalls the people whom the star stepped on during his ascent.

★

Did you catch the name of this film (and *that* summary)? If you missed the title, *Fabulous!* shall repeat it: *The Oscar.* Well, there you go. Now, it would seem that based on even the slightest and most specious amount of understanding and information anyone would have about gay men (regardless of whether you are one or not) that the reason why this is a *Fabulous!* film would need no explanation whatsoever. It would be like asking why birds fly or fish swim. Well, all right, maybe a bit is necessary. But, mind you, the rationale will only rile those who believe behavior can't always be predetermined. (Sure it can.) However, to simply postulate (although *Fabulous!* knows it is presumptive) gay men are all

cinematically inclined
competitively minded
winner fixated

Combine all three focuses into one place and guess what you get—*bingo!*—Oscar time, baby!

Back to our feature presentation.

Since there can be no doubt now as to why a film about the "all-costs" drive, desire, and determination to win one of these luscious little gold men is a "queer" killer, are there any remaining problems? Yes, and *Fabulous!* will quickly mention the movie is nowhere to be found (no doubt caught in some rights hell!). Basically, to view it you have to be driven, desirous, and determined. But for any film fan the result is worth the effort, if only for the chance to see a movie from the "annals" of Hollywood so excretingly entertaining that it is the gay camp equivalent to winning a year's worth of roughage.

But you know what smells funniest about this classic piece of crap? Tinseltown took a premise so mired in our admiration and presented it without the sight of a single sissy. Can you imagine a movie about a male star's scratching, clawing, and sleeping his way to the top (in the snooty, selfish role of Frankie Fane solidly played by Stephen Boyd) and there's not a "sister" to be seen anywhere? That's like the anomaly of the heterosexual florist: not possible! However, this is just where Hollywood was being itself by keeping things "straight," presumably so that none would be offended by the finished product. At least the original novelist (yes, it actually came from a book with words!), Richard Sale, wrote *gaily* about one of Fane's fellow acting nominees, Brett Chichester, who was, you guessed it, English! Oh, can there be no shame?

★

Just three of Oscar's gayest moments:
• A rare onscreen appearance by designer Edith Head.
• Milton Berle, as agent Kappy Kapstetter. Krazy!
• Jean Hale, as egotistical actress Cheryl Barker. Woof!

"You finally made it, Frankie! Oscar night! And here you sit on top of a glass mountain called 'success.'"

Above: Spoken in voice-over by Hymie Kelly (Tony Bennett) as he thinks back on the rise to the top of his abusive friend, actor Frankie Fane (Stephen Boyd). *Right:* Fane physically and mentally departing the company of sometime lover, talent scout Sophie Cantaro (Eleanor Parker). Everett

1940. MGM (AAN). Directed by George Cukor (AAN). Starring Katharine Hepburn (AAN), Cary Grant, James Stewart (AA), Ruth Hussey (AAN), John Howard, Roland Young, John Halliday, Mary Nash, and Virginia Weidler.

★

The basic story: A beautiful but snippy socialite is set to marry for the second time. But before her nuptials take place, she is revisited by her ex-husband, a tabloid reporter, and a photographer. The occasion is spoiled, but in the end the bride-to-be is saved from herself.

★

The bad news first: somewhat unavoidably, if one is putting together a book on the classics of "queer" cinema, one runs the risk of bringing up things that aren't always the most pleasant to think about. Curiously, for a film so nice to look at on the outside *Philadelphia* happens to be one of those "Pandora's box–like" movies.

To explain, let us begin with some background. As a young boy, it is often the gay youth who stays close to home while others go out to play. (Remember, the word used is "often," not always!) However, time is far from wasted by our little lad out of the sunshine. Facing the television in his cozy domicile, he wisely whiles away the hours watching countless well-mannered movies, and these help to teach him life's finer points (which he couldn't possibly get running roughshod in the rain or horsing around in the dirt). Theoretically, television acts as a school of deportment, and we are, not surprisingly, the most apt pupils.

Unfortunately, grown gay men may use good manners gleaned so glamorously in the wrong way, as when we "put on airs" and make others, frequently our own brothers, feel bad for not acting the same. Certain films feed on this propensity toward pretension by being just the type we are supposed to like—and therein lies the *Philadelphia* problem. Like caviar, the movie appeals to discriminating palates, but it can leave a bad taste in the mouths of some who can't get past that they are just salty fish eggs. Of course, this also rankles the nerves of those who know better and believe we should just shut up and eat them because they are there. Rather harsh, isn't it?

But now the good news: ironically, the dilemma of *Philadelphia*'s central character, Tracy Lord (a crisp Katharine Hepburn) is a close conundrum to the above. She is introduced as a beautiful yet cold, "goddesslike" woman, who knows too well the riches of the world—but only from the monied view of a Main Line family. She strides about wittily but not wisely, too high up on her horse to see that her affluent attitude shows no real grace or gratitude. But by the film's end she is brought back down to earth by this life lesson learned: expecting perfection cannot bring the happiness that accepting imperfection can. Amen to that!

★

The "story" of Philadelphia:

At the time this *Story* was being filmed, Katharine Hepburn was considered "poison" at the box office. However, just a short while earlier, playwright Phillip Barry had written this expressly with Kate in mind. Playing the role of Tracy Lord on Broadway, Hepburn was gifted with a great hit. Wisely, she bought the film rights, and with this Cukored version found herself back among Hollywood's front ranks.

"What's this room? I've forgotten my compass."

Above: Spoken sarcastically by newsphotographer Elizabeth Imbry (Ruth Hussey) to her tabloid collaborator, reporter Macaulay Connor (Jimmy Stewart). *Left:* C. K. Dexter Haven (Cary Grant) and his ex-wife, Tracy Lord (Katharine Hepburn), are joined by Connor and Imbry. Everett

Pillow Talk

1959. Universal. Directed by Michael Gordon. Starring Rock Hudson, Doris Day (AAN), Tony Randall, Thelma Ritter, Nick Adams, Julia Meade, Marcel Dalio, and Lee Patrick.

★

The basic story: A pretty decorator shares a phone line with a playboy songwriter. While hopeful that the situation will remedy itself, she is duped by the man, whom she has never met, while he is disguised as another. The composer initially attempts to make her another of his conquests, but falls in love. She, too, falls in love, but only with the man whom she thinks he is.

★

The attractions for gay men to *Pillow Talk* sound quite obvious from the beginning: the ever abstinant Doris Day plays an interior decorator (bear in mind, men, this was back when they weren't yet going by "designers") with a swellegant Upper East Side Manhattan apartment (notice the 59th Street Bridge outside her windows) that she no doubt fitted-out herself. Further, Miss Jan Morrow employs a wise housekeeper who is perpetually hammered (in a too-little-seen performance by the tersely versed Thelma Ritter), is squired by a squirrelly suitor (Tony Randall, in one of his now infamous "timid" best-friend roles) requiring an office overhaul, and is courted by a king-sized "Texan" (the never-too-big Rock Hudson) a little slow with the usual fast male moves. All the while, the heroine must contend with a "sex maniac" only because he is the other "party" of her party line (does anyone remember those?).

In the meantime, solid-as-one Rock (Hudson), playing a composer of music in the middle of writing songs for his college chum (Randall), is the mischievous mister on the other end of the party line who has the clever idea to "playact" his way into the decorator's bed with his imitation of a cowpoke who may have some real issues concerning women.

Yep, this film definitely walks the gay walk—and in order to see all the split-screen conversations, the splashy "night-out-on-the-town" montage, a jazzy lounge act (with groovy "Roly-Poly" pianist Perry Blackwell and her combo), and the sudsy side-by-side bathing scene in all their widescreen glory, you will need to watch it in letterbox. But does this gay-required viewing go too far when trying to talk our talk? Gentlemen, decide for yourself.

★

What's not so "sweet" about Talk*:*
Considered quite groundbreaking because of its humorous handling of taboo topics (mainly premarital sex), *Talk* is tame by today's explicit standards—with one exception. All's fair in this bedroom farce *unless you sleep with men.* In which case you are speaking of the worst type of man imaginable, and too vicious an accusation to even consider or continue listening to. These negative sentiments are expressed in a scene were Hudson's "real" character tries to mislead Day's by suggesting the all-too-great possibility that her beloved cowboy may be queer! The irony about this is that these thoughts are spoken by a gay favorite actress and now possibly the world's most well-known queer actor—in a Ross Hunter–produced movie about how lying can get you into trouble! Honestly, it's like taking a box of treats too tempting for us to pass by, and giving one of the sweets a secret sour middle. Confection consumers you have been warned.

"It only takes one sip of wine to know it's a good bottle."

Above: Spoken astutely by housekeeper Alma (Thelma Ritter) as courtship advice to her unmarried employer, Jan Morrow (Doris Day). *Right:* Morrow is being shown "the view" in the hotel room of Rex Stetson aka Brad Allen (Rock Hudson). Everett

Polyester

1981. New Line. Directed by John Waters. Starring Divine, Tab Hunter, Edith Massey, Mink Stole, David Samson, Joni Ruth White, May Garlington, and Ken King.

★

The basic story: A middle-class suburban housewife— possessing a heightened olfactory sense—is beset by a number of hardships, including a philandering, porn-theater-owning husband; a pregnant, unmarried daughter; and a stoned son with a foot fetish. For solace, she turns to a well-off friend and the arms of a handsome rescuer.

★

There's an odd smell around here, and it seems to be on just these two pages. Is it—*no*, that's not possible—the odor of bad taste? *Egads*, in a book for gay males, the last of well-mannered men? But that's what it is, all right. Not only that, it's a particularly ripe example of it, too. Goodness, what does this mean? Well, it means straight people aren't the only ones who can have fun with *or* create trashy cinema. Actually with *Polyester*, queer director John Waters does lowbrow lovers proud, and satisfies the sloth in all of us, while managing to parody "weepies" (a queer fave film category if there ever was one, including Waters's own) with such abandon that it makes you cry—tears of laughter.

Looking back, Waters and his *Polyester* "queen," Divine, appeared a bit like Laurel and Hardy and made a most memorable indie-film team a bit like Josef von Sternberg and Marlene Dietrich. This was perhaps their most meaningful of nine boorish collaborations (the calculated crudenesses of which movies may never see again). Hammocked between their *Pink Flamingos* (totally tasteless) and *Hairspray* (questionably taste-

less), *Polyester* was also the pair's bridge from under- to above-ground work, their attempt to link a genre (the "midnight movie") not seen as "gay" with distinct queer possibilities, and a vehicle bringing into view what was "so gay" to us but not so obvious to others. Combined, this makes *Polyester* a pivotal film in gay culture. But there's more.

While Waters's work means a lot to the success of *Polyester*, Divine's contribution may have been the bigger deal (and by that we mean huge!). One of entertainment's best *and* largest "gender illusionists," Divine's (aka Glenn Milstead's) highly visible female form definitely s-t-r-e-t-c-h-e-d the envelope, and instead of "hers" being the usual "dress-up" role (*Some Like It Hot*), the Francine Fishpaw part in *Polyester* was different: "she" was never meant or shown to be a "he." Furthermore, at no time does Waters dilute his "heroine's" heterosexuality, and, being that "she" was a "she," the character went where no "man" had gone before—including embracingly tender moments with fifties heartthrob Tab Hunter! Now that's a "reel" twist in your garters, girls!

A Polyester *"dress" option:*
Some see slipping into ladies' clothes as a step back to when all of us were seen as too fond of feminine finery. However, others are not so put out. Then just for the dressy fun of it, take a "clothes" watch of *To Wong Foo, Thanks for Everything! Julie Newmar* (1995) to see the grandest dame gathering of genuine cross-dressing queens. But don't view it for the film itself, which shows that when you put the wrong men in the wrong wardrobe (Swayze?! Snipes?!) things fast become a real drag!

"Puhr Francine. Puhr, puhr Francine."

Above: Spoken consolingly by Cuddles Kovinsky (the famously mush-mouthed Edith Massey) to her embattled best friend Francine Fishpaw (Divine). *Left: Polyester* publicity shot of Tab Hunter (Todd Tomorrow) and Divine (aka Glenn Milstead). Everett

The Red Shoes

1948. GFD-The Archers (AAN). Directed by Michael Powell and Emeric Pressburger. Starring Anton Walbrook, Marius Goring, Moira Shearer, Robert Helpmann, Léonide Massine, Albert Bassermann, Ludmilla Tcherina, and Esmond Knight.

★

The basic story: The leader of a famed ballet troupe demands total loyalty from his dancers, and, in one special case, forces a rising star to choose between her devotion to the profession and the love of one man.

★

People both straight *and* gay assume a lot of things about us. Most are probably not half true (but many not half false either!). However, one belief—*we love pretty things*—tops nearly every list. So for those who are truly appreciative, the British-made *Red* should come as a big box bursting with great visuals (looking through sparkling eyelashes), whole scenes (the *Red Shoes* ballet, obviously, but there are many more), and aurally arresting interludes (the crescendo-ed accompaniment to the "spiraling" staircase) which you will want to note in your book of future party "theme and decor" ideas. However, while the film is immensely striking, and arguably the most visually stunning ever made, *Red*'s Oscar-winning look and sound has a surprising murkiness to it which underscores the motives of the characters— and is antithetical to the beautiful, pristine world of ballet.

This somewhat grimy edge also points up aesthetic differences between English- and American-produced movies, which some suspect would turn us away from Anglofare. But this is not the case. Fans are actually drawn to the fantasy-cum-reality of *Red* in a way that makes it a little like watching a Technicolored therapy session. *Fabulous!* cautions that this aspect of *Shoes* may be too tight a fit for those whose personality traits include obsessive-compulsion, manic-depression, anal-retentiveness, controllingness, passive-aggression, perfectionism, jealousy, manipulation, and vanity.

But wait, it's also a film about devotion, dedication, and loyalty to the extent of dying for one's art, and is worth getting through the mental anguish just to see how long one very neurotic group of men in the so-masculine world of tu-tus and tights—with pardons to ballerinas Shearer and Tcherina (in their Jacques Fath gowns!)— can go without clawing each other's eyes out (but it comes close with Helpmann and Massine) or suffering from nervous breakdowns, which all but happens, brilliantly, with maniacal Boris Lermontov (Walbrook) the ballet's *empress*-ario.

★

A mismatched Shoes *pairing:*
For one quick way to see filmmaking's obvious dissimilarities when "crossing the pond," try watching *Red* alongside a very sanitized Hollywood musical production on a very close queer subject, *Hans Christian Andersen* (1952), starring a so-dandy Danny Kaye.

Five more films for fans of gaily attractive cinema:

★

Black Narcissus (1947)
Cleopatra (1963)
Great Expectations (1946)
Nicholas and Alexandra (1971)
Restoration (1995)

"Nothing matters but the music!"

Above: Spoken as a mantra by troupe leader Boris Lermontov (Anton Walbrook) to rising-star ballerina Victoria Page (Moira Shearer). *Right:* Julian Craster (Marius Goring) surprises his wife, Victoria, on the night of her encore performance of the *Red Shoes* ballet, with Lermontov goading her on to perform. Everett

1983. Geffen. Directed by Paul Brickman. Starring Tom Cruise, Rebecca De Mornay, Joe Pantoliano, Richard Masur, Bronson Pinchot, Kevin Anderson, Curtis Armstrong, Nicholas Pryor, Janet Carroll, and Bruce A. Young.

★

The basic story: While his parents are away on vacation, a good-looking high schooler makes hesitant plans to remedy his sexual inexperience. Once successful, he seeks to erotically enlighten others by venturing into a business with old friends and his new acquaintances.

★

There is a scene that plays early in the setup of this film which is so closely symbolic of a gay youth's own coming-of-age story that if they tried remaking it today *Business* might be too risky a venture. No, it is not the time when the black transvestite hooker comes a-knockin' on the door of white-boy upper-middle-class America. And no, it is not the mesmerizing "Is he doing what I think he's doing?" moment when the handsome-and-horny antihero takes matters well in hand. Nor is it "Mr. Home Alone's" super-sexy-in-white-socks-slide-dance-and-hump-the-sofa routine. Although all are key scenes, the *Business* clincher comes when Joel Goodsen (played by a *major* Tom Cruise) makes his "cover-my-face-with-a-mask-to-hide-my-identity" phone call, while seated on the kitchen floor, to call girl Lana (played by Rebecca De Mornay), which then leads him down into his own private Idaho netherworld for the next ninety-plus minutes.

The reason why this scene and basically the whole damned *Business* is so metaphorically "gay" for our viewers (of any age, really) is that the hesitancy, guilt, shame, anticipation, excitement, joy, and elation are the exact same emotions we each go through when taking tentative first steps alone into our own brave new gay world. This queer identification to *Risky* is further aided and abetted by the son's original characterization as being the goody-two-shoes boy whom anyone can trust, who, in his sexual desperation and frustration, quickly sets up an essentially illegal business that runs like a private club known only to members, which he anxiously tries keeping a secret from his parents.

What's Business *really about:*
Risky made Cruise a very big star, and lots of credit should be given to him for playing a new male cinematic character not so much in charge of his surroundings as he is their unwitting slave (boy-toy), and one who effectively changed the perception, personalities, and pretty faces of all young male stars to come, including Pitt, Reeves, Depp, and others. As to any other matters, *Fabulous!* asks is it anybody's business?

Since terrific Tom opened the movie's doors, many a handsome and sensitive young man has cruised right into a theater near you, including the following:*

★

Orlando Bloom in *Pirates of the Caribbean* (2003)
James Franco in *James Dean* (TV, 2001)
Jared Leto in *Prefontaine* (1997)
Tobey MacGuire in *Wonder Boys* (2000)
Luke Wilson in *Legally Blonde* (2001)

* check back with *Fabulous!* in a few to see where they stand

---

"It's what you want. It's what every white boy off the lake wants."

Above: Spoken smartly by black transsexual prostitute Jackie (Bruce Young) to Joel Goodsen (Tom Cruise) at the door of his suburban Chicago home. *Left: Business* publicity still of Cruise. Kobal

A Room with a View

1985. Cinecom (AAN). Directed by James Ivory (AAN). Starring Helena Bonham Carter, Julian Sands, Daniel Day-Lewis, Maggie Smith (AAN), Denholm Elliott (AAN), Simon Callow, Rupert Graves, and Judi Dench.

★

The basic story: A young Englishwoman, visiting Italy with her chaperone, encounters a fellow countryman and his gallant, attractive son—with whom she falls in love. Back at home, she must decide between marriage to a safe and reserved suitor or the dashing newcomer, who has changed her entire perspective on life.

★

On the outside, *Room* looks like it has lots to offer the fabulous filmgoer in search of a pleasant way to spend a couple of hours. It's a period piece (always good for a gay lark or two), but not so finite that it feels stuck in the past. There is also the hint of travel in the title—and you know how we love to do that! But truly, inside this *Room* is where the most compelling queer sights of all are kept.

Room's *First Gay View*

Room enhances the ideal gay goal of "*to thine own self be true*" by being a whole grandiloquent look on the subject. The main character, Charlotte Honeychurch (Helena Bonham Carter), is shown moving toward a safe but likely unhappy life. Her dilemma: to find true fulfillment she must take the risk of accepting who she is. *Room*, by first not and then finally showing the "view," further implies that the whole world is full of happiness, but only for those willing to take it for what it is, the often pretty with the sometimes ugly. (A

poignant irony to this is that author E. M. Forster, upon whose 1908 novel of the same name this film was based, was never able to accept his own homosexuality, and could only have his gayest work, *Maurice*, published posthumously for fear of reprisals.)

Room's *Second Gay View*

Upon *Room*'s mid-1980s release, the country was in a Reagan-era conservative overhaul (in response to the too-liberal-1970s Carter era), which was rather obvious by the popularity of overly macho action stars like Arnold and Sly. So it was against these traditionalist titans that Merchant and Ivory's sweet film came into view. And the gracious gentlemen who would be doing the looking? It, too, was obvious. (Another poignant irony: neither producer Merchant nor director Ivory—whom *Room* brought to our attention—was then out about their own orientations. Fortunately, neither had to wait too long to impart the welcome revelations.)

Room's *Third Gay View*

Room also showed viewers three rather good-looking examples of potential gay mates: Julian Sands, as *caring* George Emerson, the ideal "homo-hero"; Rupert Graves, as *carefree* Freddy Honeychurch, the piano-playing brother clearly besotted by his sister's suitor; and Daniel Day-Lewis (with another of those poshly extended English names), as *careful* Cecil Vyse, whose temperance may make him a touch too tepid for some tastes. But maybe not.

"He's the sort who can't know anyone intimately, least of all a woman."

Above: Spoken advisingly by George Emerson (Julian Sands) about his rival, Cecil Vyse (Daniel Day-Lewis), to his love, Lucy Honeychurch (Helena Bonham Carter). *Right:* George and Lucy meet clandestinely in the meadow while on a field trip. Kobal

136

1968. Paramount. Directed by Roman Polanski. Starring Mia Farrow, John Cassavetes, Ruth Gordon (AA), Sidney Blackmer, Patsy Kelly, Ralph Bellamy, Maurice Evans, Emmaline Henry, and Charles Grodin.

★

The basic story: A pair of newlyweds move into a foreboding Manhattan apartment house whose odd inhabitants hint at the place's dark history. One elderly couple, in particular, become the newcomers' quick friends, and soon the man's fledgling acting career takes off and his wife becomes pregnant. But while he seems happy, she grows ever more suspicious of her surroundings.

★

Not every film in *Fabulous!* has to be obviously "gay." *The devil you say?! Rosemary*, with no clearly discernible queer characters or story elements, is one of those gay-popular cinematic oddities—or is it? The only problem—*dammit all to hell*—is that what may make this film into a favorite may be an abstraction of the filmmaker's intentions and a reason hard to defend. (You know what? So is what allows half the films into this book!) What is this damned thing that *Fabulous!* thinks brings *Baby* to gay attentions, anyway?

S-T-Y-L-E!

Before dismissing this as a random excuse, remember how important this sensibility is assumed to be for our kind. Again, *assumed.* And yes, it may make us sound rather superficial, but since Rosemary just happens to be a very, very stylish "girl," we happen to love her to death. Really. However, here is some queer help to convince you otherwise of the sometimes conniving ways *Fabulous!* sneaks pictures inside for a peek (which you may have to catch on a second go-round because the film's so slick you may miss them the first time!):

• Rosemary resides not only in New York City (the greatest gay-fave locale) but deeply within the Dakota, a Manhattan landmark, and the first stop on any queer tour of Big Apple abodes!

• Model-thin Mia (with hair by Vidal Sassoon!) in her sleek pant ensembles and chic trapezes (and Ruth in her Pucci-inspired sheaths) buys so-sexy hubby (Cassavetes)—devil that he is (and theater actor, no less!)—dress shirts that she's seen in *The New Yorker*!

• Coven leader Roman Castevet (Blackmer) has pierced ears, and the androgynous party couple is in fur *and* makeup! Such heathens!

• Those sly slurs against organized religion: "The pope is all showbiz"; a *Time* cover: "Is God Dead?"; and Rosemary's dreams. Too decadent!

• Perverse Polanski using wholesome TV actors as devil worshippers (including Hope Summers, often seen as Clara on *The Andy Griffith Show*). Simply mad!

• Finally, taking a common game, Scrabble, and making it into a ciphering tool. Clever beyond words!

Baby's *queer cousin:*

Rosemary author, Ira Levin, also penned the twisted *The Stepford Wives*, which became a favorite film, too (thanks to stars Katharine Ross, Paula Prentiss, and Tina Louise). It has since been remade and Rudin-ized (as in gay play- and screenwriter Paul) with also-fave actors Nicole Kidman and Matthew Broderick.

"He has his father's eyes."

Above: Spoken with horrific honesty by the leader of devil worshippers, Roman Castevet (Sidney Blackmer), to Rosemary Woodhouse (Mia Farrow), upon the discovery of her still-living infant. *Left:* Rosemary washing dishes with nosy neighbor Minnie Castevet (Ruth Gordon), while both their husbands smoke and chat in the next room. Kobal

Sabrina

1954. Paramount. Directed by Billy Wilder (AAN). Starring Audrey Hepburn (AAN), Humphrey Bogart, William Holden, John Williams, Walter Hampden, Martha Hyer, Joan Vohs, Marcel Dalio, Francis X. Bushman, and Ellen Corby.

★

The basic story: Sent to school in Paris, a chauffeur's daughter returns home a beautiful sophisticate and becomes the center of attention for the two wealthy brothers who own the estate where she grew up.

★

First, two words: Audrey Hepburn. Second, three more words: We love her. Third, a question: Why? The answer: because she *is* Audrey, arguably the most beautiful star, outside and inside, ever to grace the screen.

But why is Hepburn such a *gay* favorite?

One way to figure that out is to use *FIT* (remember, the *Fabulous!* Identification Theory?) which, by allowing gay men to be put in her place, makes it easy to understand the attraction. Spiritually *and* physically, she embodies all the traits of "the perfect gay male": slim, good-looking, witty, engaging, thoughtful, caring, carefree—and, above all else, a clotheshorse! Consequently, unlike actresses from Bette to Meryl, female stars whom we admire greatly and in whose work we all see many parts of ourselves, Audrey is the one we would most want to be like, onscreen *and* in real life.

However, the main concern of *Fabulous!* is film, and out of her many roles *Sabrina* was chosen most gay-admired. But why? Well, of the choices, all but this one had reasons why they did *not* fully epitomize the queer essence of this lovely star. *Par example:* though she won the Oscar for *Roman Holiday* (1953) and her role was a royal treat, in many ways she was still a princess, not yet a queen; in *Funny Face* (1957) she was beyond compare, but the film itself was too couture haughty; in *Breakfast at Tiffany's* (see page 55) she sparkled, but by then was already well known as the rarest of jewels; and of her *My Fair Lady* (see page 119) she was much more, but her casting was judged *un*-fair.

So, on and on *Fabulous!* toiled until *Sabrina* waltzed by and it was obvious that the essential Audrey had been found, and here are three gay reasons why it was thought so: first, it is an exceptionally well-made movie (so good that it was remade, awfully, and a perfect example why some originals should be left alone) with an outstanding A-list director (Wilder) and co-stars, William Holden and Humphrey Bogart (though why Audrey, as *Sabrina*, would choose Bogey over Bill in the end is beyond queer comprehension); second, the "Cinderella-esque" story was timed perfectly for her career, helping to solidify Audrey's growing standing as the ultimate *objet d'amour* for charming lads and lasses (who believed in fairy godmothers and pumpkins becoming carriages); third, and this is may be the most gay-relevant reason of all, it brought Hepburn together with couturier Hubert Givenchy, thereafter placing her permanently on the catwalks in our designer-decorated hearts and minds.

★

Sabrina's "clothes" controversy:
This film brought famed designer Edith Head one of her eight Oscars for "best costumes." However, upon accepting the award, Edie deliberately did not thank Mssr. Givenchy for his *haute* contributions. Bad girl!

"Life was pleasant among the Larrabees, for this was as close to heaven as one could get on Long Island."

Above: Spoken as part of the film's opening narration by Sabrina Fairchild (Audrey Hepburn). *Right: Sabrina* publicity still of William Holden (David Larrabee) and Hepburn. Everett

1932. Paramount (AAN). Directed by Josef von Sternberg (AAN). Starring Marlene Dietrich, Clive Brook, Anna May Wong, Warner Oland, and Eugene Palette.

★

The basic story: A train bound for Shanghai containing a small group of eccentric travelers makes its way through a country engaged in civil war. En route, they are stopped by a rebel leader who keeps one of them hostage while negotiating for his release with another.

★

Every film in *Fabulous!* is here for a reason. Whether it is obvious or not, each movie makes a point about who we are (or who we *think* we are), what makes us tick, and what makes us talk among ourselves. In some of the selections, the gay hook is as pronounced as a pink polka-dot bow tie. For instance, "acceptance" (or looking to "fit in"), a common theme, is usually as easy to read as a billboard. However, in some movies finding the reason is like trying to determine the true definition of gayness, which is almost an impossibility; the essence or mood of a film is there, but often cannot be spelled out in precise language, and *Fabulous!* found that *Shanghai* was as definite an example of the undefinable yet overpowering gay film fan's fascination with a single film.

Storywise, it concerns a "fallen woman" (Dietrich) traveling with an equally descended companion—the sensational Anna May Wong (with the cliché dagger in hand)—on board a train occupied by passengers wishing to have nothing to do with persons of their sunken status. But while one can see that the "outcast" aspect to the tale would be of interest to us, making this our supreme connection to *Express* is an easy out and an oversimplification of its real gay attraction. But saying that we love *Shanghai* just because it is glamorous, moody, and sexy (in a way only possible because it was pre-code) and because it stars a glamorous, moody actress (whose sexual ambiguity, among other things, makes her a favorite) does not do it proper justice either.

The way *Fabulous!* wants to explain our attraction to *Shanghai* is by likening the film (and its star) to a glowing light and by making us little june bugs in the summer night. We are drawn to the film's "glow" because that is what little june bugs do—fly to the light. However, the attractive glow *Shanghai* casts is not such a pure and unadulterated occurrence, and therefore using it as our sole reason also has its holes. Basically, its radiance is a deliberate manipulation of the cinematographer's art (Lee Garmes, AA). Which, in particular, turns Dietrich into a blaze of white fire that smoldered almost violently within her frame of Travis Banton black feathers.

A-ha! That's it! Let's really be honest here. It's all about that *devoon* dark plumage. Now when was the last time you saw that in a film? Or a steamer trunk? And what a knockout wardrobe this downtrodden dame has, huh? Admit it, *sugarplum*, the gay reason why we run to catch this *Express* train are Lily's veils, the hats (and boxes), the jewelry, the dresses, and the rest of the ravishing raiments! But honey, just how many changes of clingy clothes does one need when crossing through a country engaged in civil war? And what does one wear to an interrogation held by a sweaty despot? The dress with the Peter Pan collar that makes you look ladylike?

"It took more than one man to change my name to Shanghai Lily."

Above: Spoken as a confessional of sorts, by Shanghai Lily (Marlene Dietrich) to her one-time paramour Capt. Donald Harvey (Clive Brook). *Left:* Lily and Donald at the station after their train adventure ends. Kobal

Sitting Pretty

1948. Twentieth Century-Fox. Directed by Walter Lang. Starring Clifton Webb (AAN), Maureen O'Hara, Robert Young, Richard Haydn, Louise Allbritton, and Ed Begley.

★

The basic story: A young married couple mistakenly hires a man as their three boys' live-in sitter. Though the pair is hesitant to keep him employed, he convinces them with his manner and experience. However, his stay still sets tongues wagging throughout their small town.

★

Fabulous! is not going to say *Pretty* is any gay man's favorite movie (but it's so darling it could be) or say it is a film we should love (but could, easily). However, in a book filled with films focused on our experience, because *Sitting* covers a large area—where gay men *were* and where we *are*—it was given a seat.

Pretty is so gay, actually, viewers may puzzle how it is that Hollywood made this "fairy tale" in the first place. But *Sitting* was just the kind of charmingly gay-innuendoed family fare the film capital did make, often and quite well. But still, considering *Pretty*'s premise, you wonder if anyone noticed this: an unmarried, older man hires himself out as a babysitter (although "nanny" seems more suitable) and conceitedly claims to be savvy on every subject any most-civilized man should know about; then, this most genteel of gentlemen, who, mind you, doesn't like children especially, turns out to be an author writing a "tell-all" book about the community—Hummingbird Hill—outing them as gossips, hypocrites, and phonies!

But even gayer things appear after a *Pretty* sitting and point out the part about the "where" of today's gay man mentioned at the start of this summary. Frankly, if someone wanted to remake this picture now it is doubtful the road ahead would be a pretty one. Why? Because one of two major changes involving the lead, Mr. Lynn Belvedere (and yes, Lynn did have his own eighties TV show), would have to occur before anyone would seriously consider the proposition. Either the character would have to come out completely—in which case, the idea of letting an older gay male watch *and* bathe very young male children, among other intimacies, would probably be denounced by every conservative watchdog group from here to kingdom come—or Lynn would have to be completely heterosexualized, becoming Len. Unfortunately this would not fly either, because no one would buy the thought of a grown straight man as a kidsitter (unless, of course, they were Tony Danza's agents).

Another *Pretty* queerness is that despite being gay as a goose, Clifton Webb became a leading man *and* the object of many women's desires (in the Liberace vein, if you get the drift) thanks to his *Sitting* success. But just to play it safe, *Pretty*'s producers brought in nelly support—the nosy neighbor horticulturalist Mr. Appleton (Haydn)—to try and make Webb look more manly! As if! A *Fabulous!* question of the moment: Could someone so obviously gay as Webb be able to work today? Yes, but only if Ian McKellan was booked. (As you know, there is only room for one at a time.)

A fitting Sitting *companion:*
Monty Woolley as curmudgeonly critic Sheridan Whiteside in *The Man Who Came to Dinner* (1942).

"Only an idiot is completely happy anywhere."

Above: Spoken acerbically by "genius" Mr. Lynn Belvedere (Clifton Webb) to the gossipy man he loathes, Mr. Appleton (Richard Haydn). *Right:* Belvedere informs his employers, Harry and Tacey King (Robert Young and Maureen O'Hara), that the reason why they could not enter his room to snoop was because he had changed the door's lock. Kobal

1959. United Artists. Directed by Billy Wilder (AAN). Starring Jack Lemmon (AAN), Tony Curtis, Marilyn Monroe, Joe E. Brown, George Raft, Pat O'Brien, Nehemiah Persoff, Joan Shawlee, and Dave Barry.

★

The basic story: Two musicians witness a gangland slaying in Depression-era Chicago. With no money or other options, they escape to Florida as players in an all-female band—with themselves in full drag. Once they arrive their troubles are far from over: the gangsters are hot on their heels, and both men have gotten into relationships under their false identities.

★

No movie book needs to remind readers about how great a film *Hot* is. They already know what an impact it made as an odd mix of sex and violence in a farce that was way too racy for some at the time (the last desperate days of the fifties) and how it continues making things "hot" today by surpassing in quality any current contenders. But maybe a look at *Hot* from the outsider's point of view can add something that you haven't read, seen, or heard.

Imagine what gay viewers must have thought when seeing *Hot* for the first time. Yes, Curtis and Lemmon are just two men in drag (and no, putting men in dresses may get our attention but it does not instantly win our favor). However, extending their "dressed" circumstances through the whole film made it like watching an alternate lifestyle (more so than a single-scene gimmick) and that—along with the identity crisis factor: "What makes a man a man and a woman a woman?"—made all the difference. Additionally, while the *Hot* character

team expressed difficulty dressing and carrying themselves off as women, they never mentioned distaste at the idea—not really—giving the impression that doing so was all right and after a while even comfortable (Lemmon as Daphne toward the film's end).

However, one of the main reasons why they were able to pull this off is because as "drag queens"—in appearance to the entire audience—Tony and Jack were terrible looking and obviously *not* women (actually they shot so unattractively that Wilder changed from color to black-and-white film). That they were still clearly men also made them acceptable to mainstream viewers (like their own "insider's joke"). Had the pair been too gender successful, *Hot* would have been much harder for them to take. (Curious how straight people can handle *Hot* as long as they know they're guys in dresses, isn't it?) The just-under-the-surface maleness of the pair also turns Marilyn's character Sugar Cane (for which she won a Golden Globe) into something of a screen "fruit fly" who uses her two "big sisters"—with their "broad shoulders" and "flat chests"—as confidantes for her thoughts and feelings about the "opposite" sex.

Five more men pulled from the *Fabulous!* "drag bag":

★

Leslie Cheung in *Farewell, My Concubine* (1993)
Cary Grant in *I Was a Male War Bride* (1949)
Dustin Hoffman in *Tootsie* (1982)
Nathan Lane in *The Birdcage* (1996)
Robin Williams in *Mrs. Doubtfire* (1993)

"Nobody's perfect."

Above: Spoken as a last attempt to correct misconceptions by Daphne aka Jerry (Jack Lemmon) to Osgood Fielding III (Joe E. Brown), whom "she" had planned on marrying. *Left:* Daphne and friend Josephine aka Joe (Tony Curtis) plan a hasty departure from their south Florida sanctuary. Kobal

The Sound of Music

1965. Twentieth Century-Fox (AA). Directed by Robert Wise (AA). Starring Julie Andrews (AAN), Christopher Plummer, Eleanor Parker, Richard Haydn, Peggy Wood (AAN), Anna Lee, Charmian Carr, Heather Menzies, Nicholas Hammond, Duane Chase, Angela Cartwright, Debbie Turner, Kym Karath, and Marni Nixon.

★

The basic story: Based on a true story, a novitiate leaves the nunnery to become the governess of a retired naval officer's large family whom she beguiles while the world rages at the beginnings of war.

★

In a gay perfect world would all fathers be handsome, wealthy, retired-at-forty sea captains *and* sexy folk-singing guitarists, and would the symphonic strains of a full orchestra magically produce itself during normal everyday activities, like, say, a sterlingly performed puppet show—for which there was no discernible time to practice (and, for that matter, would we all have our own puppet theaters)—in our own lakeside manse's mirrored ballrooms? Bewildering thoughts like these, and more, come up when watching *Music*, and, in various states, occur when watching any musical. Such is the numbing effect the genre has on the usual complex state of the human mind. Beware.

For years gay men have been conjoined to musicals like something out of old Siam. But the times they have been a-changin', and as the category fell from favor we, too, felt a lessening of interest. However, complete musical separation may never be likely. For what cleaves us to them might be at the heart of what makes us gay. Muse on that for a moment, while considering an explanation, which may best be seen and heard in *Sound.*

Gents (and ladies), most musicals are simply corny, and *Music* is as do-re-medial as they come, but it also lyrically sings of their gay allure: "music hath charms to soothe the savage breast." Does not the dour dad in *Music* come over to the softer side of things the minute he begins to sing? *Fabulous!* ventures that it's the softening effect of men singing that takes their sting away, and according to our precepts the world is too strict a heterocentric patriarchy. If this does not do the trick, just note that the next time you hear of a musical gone the "hard-rock" route, the sound is typically less sweet.

But there is another reason why gay men are particularly taken with this musical above and beyond many others. Just supposing that all gay men are like their mothers (and remember, this theory is based on a gross assumption that may cause some to run screaming into the hills), mightn't we be genetically predisposed to like *Music*, the *mater* of all mother-loved musicals? Note: Moms choose *Music* because it's long on melodious family and short on glamorous ostentation.

If you don't care for striking a matriarchal tone maybe these last chords will sound better: Maria (Julie Andrews) is a "sings all the time" misfit, crafty with a sewing needle, and basically just looking for a place to fit in and call home. And, as bonuses, the beautiful Baroness Schraeder (Parker) and Uncle Max (Haydn) are covert gay characters because: she is clever, conceited, wears beautiful clothes taken from her own design house, and, most connivingly, is ready to send the kiddies she so dislikes to boarding school the moment she is wed; and he is a childless, unmarried musical-act producer.

"After all, the wool from the black sheep is just as warm."

Above: Spoken by Sister Margaretta (Anna Lee) in defense of errant novitiate Maria (Julie Andrews) to a casual grouping of nuns in the convent courtyard. *Right:* Maria consoles youngest daughter, Gretl Von Trapp (Kym Karath), on a rainy night. Kobal

1954. Warner Bros. Directed by George Cukor. Starring Judy Garland (AAN), James Mason (AAN), Charles Bickford, Jack Carson, Tommy Noonan, Lucy Marlow, and Amanda Blake.

★

The basic story: An alcoholic movie actor whose celebrity is on the wane becomes the mentor—and husband—of an unknown singer whom he helps to become a star.

★

Are you the type who believes all gay men are "musical-loving, glammed-out, over-the-top, A-list-wannabe, star-obsessed, melodramatic queens"? Well, if you are, *Fabulous!* has something it wants you to see. From beginning to end, *Star* is the one movie that has it all—jeez, it's practically a queer cinephile's Christmas wish list that literally rolls out the "red carpet"—and is as classic an embodiment of so-called "gay" entertainment as you can get. But just remember this, *Fabulous!* does not say that watching *Star* holds the answers to all your problems or that movie fandom queerly starts and stops with Judy Garland. (Because in either case it isn't *really* true, but close.)

Speaking of little Miss Frances Gumm (aka Garland, the earliest years), because her name in recent association anywhere with the word "gay" is enough to send some sissies out in the streets shouting "Tired!" and "Old!," *Fabulous!* finds coming to her defense necessary. Fortunately, *Star* has what's needed on celluloid to prove, hopefully once and for all, why it was that she became so beloved by gay men to begin with and why it is that she should remain so. Produced by her then-husband, Sid Luft, *Star* was Garland's

movie comeback (after being fired a few years earlier from her home studio, MGM), and while it isn't the objective of *Fabulous!* to critique individual roles, per se, her poignant performance in a part eerily reflective of her own life was pictured perfection. End of discussion. (Surprisingly, Garland still lost the Oscar she was most predicted to win—and most fans still find it a contentious outcome—but she did get a Golden Globe.)

However, the inimitable Garland alone is not what makes *Star* the great film many gays (and straights) claim it to be. It only becomes one when she, along with James Mason, her other co-stars (especially those in the smaller, atmospheric parts), the director, the script, the score, the sets, the costumes, etc., are placed into this $6 million production (that looks like they spent sixty), which encompasses all the finer points of finessed filmmaking that those who love the medium say are essential to making a movie into an experience. To reiterate, perhaps no other motion picture has come as close to cinematic gay heaven. Hallelujah!

★

Five shimmering "stars" in *A Star Is Born*:

The song to always remember:
  Garland's "The Man That Got Away"
The speaking voice you wish you had:
  That of James Mason
The scene with the most tension:
  "Norman Interrupts Vicki's Oscar Moment"
The shot to end all shots:
  Vicki-Esther-Judy "frames" herself (see left)
The line to live your life by:
  "Don't settle for the little dream, go on to the big one."

"Hello, everybody. This is Mrs. Norman Maine."

Above: Spoken resolutely by Vicky Lester aka Esther Blodgett aka Mrs. Norman Maine (Judy Garland) to a large benefit audience, after the death of her actor husband. *Left:* Vicky re-creating the close-up shot from the day's rehearsal of a musical number for her husband, Norman Maine (James Mason). Everett

Suddenly, Last Summer

1959. Columbia. Directed by Joseph L. Mankiewicz. Starring Katharine Hepburn (AAN), Elizabeth Taylor (AAN), Montgomery Clift, and Mercedes McCambridge.

★

The basic story: A rich widow whose son recently passed away promises a doctor that she will fund his expansion plans, but only if he performs a lobotomy on her own niece, whom she believes became unstable and a danger to those around her after the man died.

★

A book on "our" movies would be incomplete without including at least one work by famed playwright Tennessee Williams. But the inclusion of this great voice of prior gay generations creates an immediate problem. To many, young *and* old, Williams's work represents our dark oppressive past and they would rather not be reminded of it again. The point is well taken, but *Fabulous!* believes that in order to fully grasp the queerness of movies one must, along with the good, consider the bad and the ugly, too. However, respectful of the situation, *Fabulous!* will refrain from using the word "favorite" and notes that the glam tone of the book will be placed on temporary hold.

Of course, the next problem, in regard to films of Williams's tales, is in choosing which "best" illustrates what the time regarded as the "worst" type of humankind. Heavens! However, when reviewing the roster, *Fabulous!* realized that while it was possible to find less-distressing depictions of closeted, self-hating fairies, it would serve our purposes better to pick a flick that most shockingly contrasts gay life then with now, so that we, out and proud, can appreciate the indignity those before us

endured. (No, not a terribly fun thought, but a good way to get perspective.)

With that as the goal, *Suddenly* quickly became the most offensively obvious, and not just because it was the most egregious example. In its outlandishness, *Summer* almost makes the demoralization fathomable. Here we have three actors, among the biggest stars ever, running around an insane asylum acting crazier than the inmates. Okay, Monty doesn't do any screaming (or look his best, as this was well after his infamous accident), but Hepburn and Taylor screech about like the same carnivorous bird-like boys shown allegorically descending upon Sebastian—seen only in flashback, the "dear" departed son with a sick secret that cost him his life—and that's a damned wonderful sight to watch. It should also be noted that the outrageous immorality in *Summer* repelled many conservatives, which we love, but we hate that most of the distaste for the film came because of our insertion into the plot.

If *Suddenly* is too much for some delicate eyes to tender, consider these five other Tennessee tempests:

★

Baby Doll (1956)
Silly now, but censors then were wary of Carroll Baker!

Cat on a Hot Tin Roof (1958)
Sin-sational Liz Taylor and Paul Newman with a past

The Roman Spring of Mrs. Stone (1961)
Bad Beatty, great Lenya and Leigh (but is hers a male role?)

A Streetcar Named Desire (1951)
A buff Brando, Vivien Leigh, and her "kind" strangers

Sweet Bird of Youth (1962)
Shirtless Paul and perfect Page (but is hers as above?)

"And this you won't believe!"

Above: Spoken desperately by Catherine Holly (Elizabeth Taylor) to Dr. Cukrowicz (Montgomery Clift) when describing the tormented death of her beloved cousin, Sebastian. *Right:* Catherine confronts the aunt who had her committed for brain surgery, Mrs. Venable (Katharine Hepburn), while the doctor looks on. Everett

1950. Paramount (AAN). Directed by Billy Wilder (AAN, AA script). Starring Gloria Swanson (AAN), William Holden, Erich von Stroheim (AAN), Fred Clark, Nancy Olson (AAN), and Jack Webb.

★

The basic story: A broke and jobless screenwriter tells the story—posthumously—of how he became the kept man of a faded silent-movie queen and her reluctant accomplice in a career comeback attempt.

★

In the humble estimation of *Fabulous!*, 1950 was the movies' *très* gayest year.* Why? Well, by noting the following partial list of films from that glorious time you should come to the same queer conclusion: *All About Eve, Born Yesterday, Adam's Rib, Samson and Delilah, Annie Get Your Gun, Harvey, Caged, Cyrano de Bergerac*, Disney's *Cinderella*, the animated short *Gerald McBoing Boing*, and *Sunset Boulevard*.

Notably, the first and last features are always chosen as crowning-film jewels (not to mention always selected as gay-favorite movie gems), and one's always set against the other. That year, they were even in direct Oscar competition, each winning some, and both losing their expected Best Actress statuette to long shot Judy Holliday for *Born Yesterday*, because votes ended up split among *Eve*'s Davis and Baxter and *Sunset*'s Swanson. However, *Fabulous!* is concerned mainly with the gayness of film, and in that contest gives the prize to *Boulevard* because in many queer ways it moves even closer than *Eve* in our direction.

Take the relationship between Norma Desmond (hauntingly played by Gloria Swanson, in one of those roles gay men groove on because it's so like the star's real life) and Joe Gillis (handsomely played by hunky William Holden). Here is an "older" woman taking care of a "younger" man. At the very least, many straight men see this as too dominant a female part and too emasculating a male part. But as you should know by now, we are not so soured by power shifts based on age, sex, or money, and see theirs as quite the acceptable pairing. Further, some gay men could just as easily have accepted Norma if the role were played by a Norm—and are convinced that this gender switchability is intended queer subtext. If you think this is a stretch just to make a gay point, imagine how much queerer *Sunset* would have been had director Wilder gotten whom he originally wanted for the Gillis part: Montgomery Clift!

Then next, why not take a gay tour along with Norma on her vanity trip through *Sunset*, an embittered behind-the-scenes journey that gives viewers a hard look at the dangerous delusions of "show" business, and one that pokes and prods at everything we love (and love to see pulled down), while still taking time out to *make over* along the way to the most memorable closing (and closing line) in movie history. Wow, this sounds like a ride most of us wouldn't dream of missing!

★

Just two of the gay "lines" crossed on the *Boulevard*:
- "Well as long as the lady's paying for it, why not take the Vicuna?" Spoken by the suit salesperson to Gillis.
- "I am. Now get off. This is more important!" Spoken by Hedda Hopper to a cop while calling in her gossip column.

---

* *Fabulous!* naturally follows the Academy Award calendar year.

"I'm richer than all this new Hollywood trash!"

Above: Spoken disgustedly by has-been actress Norma Desmond (Gloria Swanson) to her paid escort and collaborator, Joe Gillis (William Holden). *Left:* Norma informs director Cecil B. DeMille (as himself) that she cannot wait to begin work, but to remember that she never works before ten in the morning or after four in the afternoon. Everett

The Ten Commandments

"God opens the sea with a blast of his nostrils."

Above: Spoken by the old blind man (John Liljan) upon the parting of the Red Sea. *Right:* Moses (Charlton Heston), shirtless and center, discusses labor with Ramses (Yul Brynner) while also-shirtless stonecutter Joshua (John Derek), builder Baka (Vincent Price), and water girl Lilia (Debra Page) pay close attention. Kobal

1956. Paramount (AAN). Directed by Cecil B. DeMille. Starring Charlton Heston, Yul Brynner, Edward G. Robinson, Anne Baxter, Nina Foch, Yvonne DeCarlo, John Derek, H. B. Warner, Henry Wilcoxon, Judith Anderson, John Carradine, Cedric Hardwicke, Martha Scott, Vincent Price, and Debra Paget.

★

The basic story: A prince of Egypt falls out of favor with the pharaoh and is banished only to return as the messenger of God's law.

★

Hollywood is so sneaky. There was this thing—maybe you've heard of it—called "the code." It was a list of "suggestions" set down by the Hays Office, Joseph Breen, and the Catholic League of Decency of what was deemed suitable viewer content in the movies. With the power of the church (and upstanding citizens) this group was able to eliminate overt sexual activity, among other things, from being seen onscreen. If it was, the film didn't get a seal of approval, a theater, an audience, or a return on investment dollars. See how that works? But Tinseltown wanted and needed it both ways—to appease censors and please crowds with sex—so it had to get tricky and conjure ways to circumvent the system.

Many took situations and dialogue in their films—directors Wilder and Mankiewicz were two of the most adept—and made them so innuendoed that watchdogs never knew which end was up. But the answer to most of Hollywood's prurient prayers came from those who used the the Bible—a book full of salacious tales just waiting to be told—to disguise wantonness so that religious zealots could enjoy a film without guilt, while others, more churlish than churchly, could salivate over many a sweaty slave knowing that their enjoyment of such was protected by the word of God. Ah-men.

The most divinely crafty of these craftsmen was Cecil B. DeMille, and no "good book" on the subject of film, gay or straight, would be complete without one of his spectacles of biblical proportions on its pages. Fortunately, in his $13 million remake of his own silent classic, we have a film that speaks volumes about the very topic of taking licentious liberties, which "commands" the attention of any viewer looking for sexual subterfuge, but which the condemning censors seemed never able to find.

★

Ten's most commandingly gay moment:
No scene in *Ten* is as obviously gay as, say, a picnic in May. But like the goodies sure to be found in those baskets, *Ten* is stocked with dainty delicacies. You just have to do some digging to find them. However, one particular moment does jump out and queerly grab you (by the ankles and wrists!). Readers, be on the lookout for when Joshua (as acted by a pantingly pretty John Derek) is stretched and bound between two columns in the home of a whip-wielding Baka (played "queenly" and viciously by Vincent Price). It's a short sojourn between these two men, but sadomasochistically sweet and made ever more erotic when Moses (played by every gay man's favorite loincloth wearer, Charlton Heston) climbs over the wall, kills the offender with his own leather, and rescues the imperiled stonecutter from a fate worse than death.

1974. MGM. Directed by Jack Haley, Jr. Starring as narrators Fred Astaire, Bing Crosby, Gene Kelly, Peter Lawford, Liza Minnelli, Donald O'Connor, Debbie Reynolds, Mickey Rooney, Frank Sinatra, James Stewart, and Elizabeth Taylor.

★

The basic story: A documentary comprised of scenes from notable MGM musicals, narrated by the stars whose work is often featured.

★

Documentaries don't appear to number greatly on many gay men's lists of film favorites. Is that because most are *sooo* serious and we're all about having fun? Besides, aren't they all made in black-and-white? Well, you can just imagine, du-*ull.* But what would happen if one came colorfully along featuring something we all love? How about a documentary (or more apropos, *quasi*-documentary or docu-*lite*) made up entirely of the best song-and-dance scenes (though some are shamefully edited) from many of the best musicals ever made? Sort of like a two-hour-plus block's worth of videos on a fifties version of MTV—created by hundreds of the most talented choreographers, designers, musicians, directors, and, of course, singers and dancers in the business.

Actually, one's age (how old or young) may also be the main determinant in what emotional impact *Entertainment* will (or did) have on viewers. When released in 1974, *Entertainment* was meant to be a self-congratulatory fiftieth anniversary celebration—and reminder to audiences nostalgic for Hollywood's "golden age"—of what one studio (MGM) self-proclaimingly did best, the musical. Musical lovers (gay men) flocked to see—often with their mothers in tow (who were around when these films first ran)—the Jack Haley, Jr. (yes, the son of *Oz*'s Tinman) production, making it a surprise superhit that spawned two more installments—the third being possibly the best and certainly most *docu*-like.

But now is the even greater test of time for *Entertainment*. Can a retro-ish film so embraced by a whole decades-past gay generation entice younger ranks to recall musicals as fondly? Or have our latest dancers moved on, leaving the moments to fade into foot-tapping notes? Maybe a few minutes spent indulgently watching snippets will convince them to shuffle-step back where they belong. Here are five sensational segments *Fabulous!* feels may help with the persuading:

"A Pretty Girl Is Like a Melody" (*The Great Ziegfeld*, 1936)

The ballet (from *An American in Paris*, 1951)

"Get Happy" (*Summer Stock*, 1950)

"Honeysuckle Rose" (*As Thousands Cheer*, 1943)

"They Can't Take That Away from Me" (*The Band Wagon*, 1953)

Earlier kidding aside, gay men love documentaries—*really we do!*—and here are five *Fabulous!* gay-themed recommendations:

★

The Cockettes (2002)

Common Threads: Stories from the Quilt (1989, AA)

Paragraph 175 (1999)

Paris Is Burning (1990)

The Times of Harvey Milk (1984, AA)

"The next time someone says dancing is for sissies . . . "

Above: Spoken by one of *Entertainment*'s many narrators, Bing Crosby, while introducing a clip from *Seven Brides for Seven Brothers* (1954), which he further comments should prove that dance can be a *manly* endeavor. *Left:* The ballet from *An American in Paris*, featuring stars Gene Kelly and Leslie Caron, shown at its beginning. Everett

Thelma and Louise

1991. Universal. Directed by Ridley Scott (AAN). Starring Susan Sarandon (AAN), Geena Davis (AAN), Harvey Keitel, Michael Madsen, Christopher McDonald, and Brad Pitt.

★

The basic story: A waitress and a housewife set off on a weekend trip away from their dissatisfying lives and relationships with men. However, an unfortunate encounter forces the pair to run from the law.

★

Most directors have enough trouble holding things together with one general concept in their pictures, but Ridley Scott was able to combine three into his film—and pull it off quite successfully. Coincidentally, each is very gay friendly, and how splendid is that for *Fabulous!*?

Concept One: T&L *as a "Woman's" Picture*
Though Sarandon and Davis bear little physical resemblance to the tailored Tessies of forties films (the poor dears only wear jeans!), they share their earlier sisters' dreams of emancipation and go them one better with empowerment through powerful but not *too* powerful means (too emotionally or physically violent, and we would have been turned off).

Concept Two: T&L *as a "Road" Picture*
Yes, gay men love traveling, but the "road" here is symbolic of living one's life free and open. This makes *T&L*, especially, like coming out in a convertible. How snazzy! Admittedly, road films appeal to a broad spectrum of moviegoers. But that's okay, we can share the ride.

Concept Three: T&L *as a "Buddy" Picture*
In original *mano-a-mano* form, the "buddy" film is expected to be protected from our kind getting in. If we do, even accidentally, all the fun of heterosexual male bonding is spoiled. Suddenly, because of us, locker-room horseplay becomes foreplay, stare-downs become lingering looks, and Butch and Sundance go from friends to lovers. Fortunately, the gender switching in *T&L* changed those rules, allowing us full entry into this former straight-men-only club without fear.

Moving the men's character positions from the top to the bottom also allowed *T&L* to redress filmdom's typically female "plaything" role in a scene most women and gay male viewers could not forget (and one that straight men would like to!). *Fabulous!* is speaking of when Brad Pitt, in a star-making strip, changes out of his jeans and forever changes the filmgoer's view of the male form. Quite literally, it stands up as one of the single most homoerotic scenes in cinema! And for more male flesh-peddling, here are five more scenes to gaze upon:

★

Richard Gere exercising upside down
in *American Gigolo* (1980)

Steve Guttenberg rising in the water
in *Cocoon* (1985)

Dennis Quaid after being knifed
in *Suspect* (1987)

John Travolta wearing teeny-tiny black briefs
in *Saturday Night Fever* (1977)

Leonard Whiting atop the bedcovers
in *Romeo and Juliet* (1968)

"You could park a car in the shadow of his ass."

Above: Spoken lasciviously by Thelma (Geena Davis) to her cohort, Louise (Susan Sarandon), after her fling with sexy wanderer J. D. (Brad Pitt). *Right:* J. D. and Thelma get down to business in bed. Everett

1934. MGM (AAN). Directed by W. S. Van Dyke (AAN). Starring William Powell (AAN), Myrna Loy, Maureen O'Sullivan, Nat Pendleton, Minna Gombell, Porter Hall, Henry Wadsworth, William Henry, Harold Huber, Cesar Romero, Natalie Moorhead, and Edward Brophy.

★

The basic story: An amateur sleuth is asked to help clear a man accused of murder by his daughter. The man takes the case along with his wife (and dog!), but only because he finds the endeavor fun and thinks that the police are on the wrong track.

★

Here we have this bright, witty, urbane couple who live in a swanky apartment with their wirehaired fox terrier, Asta, and solve crimes with police on the side. Does this sound like a pair you might know? (Okay, maybe the crime-solving part isn't as familiar, but the rest should be.) However, before giving a complete answer *Fabulous!* would like to mention that of all of its seventy-five films *Thin* is largely the most *homo*-centric. If you are unacquainted with this term (which *Fabulous!* made up!), let us first explain all the queer nuances of cinema thusly:

Some movies are "gay friendly." Meaning they are "nice" when it comes to having us around in the audience, although we are not necessarily physically in the picture.

Some movies are "gay positive." These films (though mostly *not* seen in *Fabulous!*) typically include a gay character or theme that tries to show us in the most flattering light possible for the project itself.

Some films have a "gay" sensibility. Herein the movie's edges take on the sophisticated smoothness that only we can add to the usual roughness left by heterosexual manhandling.

Some films are "homoerotic." Bear in mind the part of the word which necessitates that a film labeled as such must have some sense of carnality. This separates it from the gay-sensible film, which mainly does not.

Some films can be "homo-centric." Finally, these are the very few movies that for all intents and purposes are *gay*, but by the simplest of disguises are covered for the general public to appear "straight."

★

So now let us go back to the question of whether you recognize the Charles couple: a childless conjoining and their well-bred dog living in a magnificent Manhattan apartment, visited upon by lots of elegant and eccentric people. However, again before answering, you should recall something else about this shrewd duo that is rather troubling. *They have quite the drinking problem.* Especially Nick, who seems forever in an alcohol-altered state of mind. While this might have seemed funny at the time (and the height of cosmopolitan behavior?), it only points out to present observers that Mr. Charles might be most unhappy about something, and drowns his subverted sorrows in drink. What, pray tell, could one in his sophisticated situation have to feel sorry or ashamed about? Readers can think further on that while claiming them now, but at their own risk.

"Oh Nicky, I love you because you know such lovely people."

Above: Spoken tongue-in-cheek by Nora Charles (Myrna Loy) to her husband, Nick Charles (William Powell). *Left:* Nick and Nora enjoy martinis with Tommy (Henry Wadsworth). Everett

Valley of the Dolls

1967. Twentieth Century-Fox. Directed by Mark Robson. Starring Barbara Parkins, Patty Duke, Susan Hayward, Paul Burke, Sharon Tate, Martin Milner, Tony Scotti, Lee Grant, Alex Davion, Charles Drake, and Naomi Stevens.

★

The basic story: A trio of beautiful young women struggle (with some success) in different areas of the entertainment business. To cope with the demands of their professional and private lives, however, each one finds refuge in drugs and alcohol.

★

There comes a time for every gay man when his own fabulousness cannot divine reasons for his exquisite being, and he must turn to the baser forms for help in understanding the true meaning of life through those eternal questions: "Who am I?" and "What am I?" And how fortunate are we, hungry and thirsty for this knowledge, but not particularly willing to work terribly hard for the answers, to have one big ol' mess of a movie that can reveal all the dirt to us?

Yes, *Valley* is truly a luxuriously indolent trip into the hazy, amphetamine-filled, undermost regions of all human existence—and don't we still love every stinking, dirty, sleazy, empty moment of it? Yeah, baby! And if given the chance, we'd invite everybody we know to join us for a gander, wouldn't we? Of course we would, because that's what friends are for. Just keep an eye on your wallet, lock up the liquor and the medicine cabinet, and hold on to your man, tight, because nothing here is off limits.

Honestly, the fact that no person, place, or thing is safe in the *Valley* is exactly why we gay men love run-

"Ted Casablancas is NOT a fag . . . and I'm the dame who can prove it!"

Above: Spoken boastingly by Neely O'Hara (Patty Duke) to her dejected husband, Mel (Martin Milner), after he expresses dismay that she is spending too much time with "that fag." *Right:* Recuperating Neely reaching for imaginary pills in the sanatorium. Kobal

ning to it for a fix. Besides, everything here seems so familiar: three "dolls" dealing with men and all working in different areas of the entertainment industry?! Well, duh! But as if that weren't enough reason to wallow, *Dolls* is perhaps the best of the worst Hollywood film has to offer in the "good start/bad finish" camp department (and you know how we love that!). Beginning with a mega-selling book, an attractive and, yes, acclaimed cast, and a noted crew, somehow things never come together in *Valley*. But the broken pieces left behind are a smash unto themselves, and here are five of the best bits every *Fabulous!* gay fan should recognize:

> **Patty Duke:** "Telethon" (and those neckbeads!)
> **Susan Hayward:** The "I'll Build My Own Tree" number*
> **Barbara Parkins:** The "Gillian Girl" commercial
> **Tony Scotti:** Convalescing in a wheelchair
> **Sharon Tate:** Breast enlargement

Without a doubt, *Dolls* is the "queen" of campy films. But before giving it the crown, *Fabulous!* asks that we take one more look at the honoree. Why is it that gay men come off as the lowest of the low in a film that's hardly highbrow (see quote)? You would think this would make *Dolls* hard for us to take. Instead, the "booze and pills" just seem to impair our better judgement and we swallow it down whole in one self-deprecating gulp.

★

*Who's the real "doll" here?:
Who dubbed for a "singing" Susan Hayward, and who was the actual thespian rumored to be inspiration for hellish Helen Lawson? See page 188 for the answers.

1973. Columbia. Directed by Sydney Pollack. Starring Barbra Streisand (AAN), Robert Redford, Bradford Dillman, Lois Chiles, Patrick O'Neal, Viveca Lindfors, and Murray Hamilton.

★

The basic story: A man and woman meet in college and fall in love despite the enormous differences in their backgrounds and ideologies. Unfortunately, the chasm between them cannot be bridged forever, and they eventually separate for good.

★

If the sadness of that short summation has already brought about the sniffles, then we're halfway home to the reasons why this "weepie" is a gay favorite. However, with all that you have learned from *Fabulous!* by now it might be too trivial to say further that gay men love *Way* simply because we can see ourselves in the roles created by Babs Streisand, the "plain-Jane" militant outsider fighting for human rights, and Bob Redford, the "glamour boy" insider who always gets by on his looks. And basically, what obvious gayness is not here to get, anyway?

However, *Fabulous!* has not included *Way* by virtue of the blatant queer charm of its two lead characters and story. *Way* was picked because its gay-preferred status (although *Fabulous!* must remind readers that such peaked many years ago) is a good example of how much like the "straight" world we really are. No kidding! However, to see this connection you must *not* look at *Way* as though it has any undeniable gay sensibility (it has some, but not as forcefully as many others). You need to watch *Way* just as an ordinary mainstream film—that

gay men happen to enjoy. This is a very important differentiation. One approach implies that queer subtleties are the main gay lure, while the other simply shows us that some attractions are universal. The next time you view *Way*, try watching it not as a gay person attempting to find gay subtext but just as a person hoping to find how similar the good and bad in life can be for all—and you will likely see it. (*Way* profound!)

But another curiousness of why *Way* is gayer than most other straight romance films is in how this picture veers from the usual too-heterosexual formula of what Hollywood commonly refers to as the "date movie." Also called a "chick flick," these are tags given to those films marketed pretty much directly to straight women. Even though gay men love pictures with women in them (actually, it's mostly a requirement), those created with such specific gender and sexual preference are often highly disliked, typically because the male lead may be too much of a "queer" put-off. But this is how the loving couple in *Way* gaily separate themselves from the others: at no time does Redford come across as "off limits" (but he's not necessarily up for grabs!) and Streisand is just so instantly simpatico that all of her films seem like open "gay" invitations.

Interestingly, that gay men were/are attracted to *Way* has never taken away from its humongous heterosexual popularity. However, again, the way things were for *Way* back then have changed somewhat drastically. When this film was released in the early seventies, labels were just beginning to be used. Now everything is marked clearly—and queerly. (Whoa, also *way* profound!)

"Oh God, please don't start a sentence with 'look'—it's always bad news."

Above: Spoken despondently by Katie Morosky (Barbra Streisand) to husband Hubbell Gardner (Robert Redford), hoping to stop his acknowledgment of the deterioration of their relationship. *Left:* Katie and Hubbell meet and eat in Manhattan while he is on leave. Kobal

What Ever Happened to Baby Jane?

1962. Warner Seven Arts. Directed by Robert Aldrich. Starring Bette Davis (AAN), Joan Crawford, Victor Buono (AAN), Anna Lee, and Anne Barton.

★

The basic story: A once famous child star, now grown up and forgotten, entertains thoughts of a comeback. However, her ambitions are slow to progress because she is the unwilling and unkind caretaker of her invalid sister—a once famous movie star—with whom she has had a long and bitter rivalry.

★

Hollywood often believes that when a movie does not succeed its failure is hinted to somewhere inside or outside of the film itself. (For example, the Sharon Stone movie titled *The Quick and the Dead*, which *quickly died* at the box office.) This makes you wonder if screenwriters delete banal sentences like "I've got a bad feeling about this" or "Things don't look good" from scripts in a last-minute dash to insure success (and, you know, they probably do). Eerily, this is not as far-fetched an idea as you might think. Just watch one bad movie, and likely there will come a line tolling its own death knell. Spooky! *Fabulous!* takes this "fortune-telling" a step further by saying a star's entire career can have one film that forever casts a negative shadow on all their contributions, no matter how stellar, and believes that happened to our babes Bette and Joan in *What Ever.*

However, don't take this as an indication that *Baby* is a failed movie. *Jane* happens to be a very good girl at entertaining, if you don't mind your broads looking a little worse for the wear. Which is precisely why doing it— even though it ended up being such a good film (and a huge sleeper hit that spawned a grand guignol film glut)—might have been a fatal move for two of our favorite females. By so unabashedly and garishly playing two has-been actresses (which mimicked low points both were experiencing in their own careers), they amply armed those in and outside of our community with ammunition to point at these icons, the oldest of the "old school," and say "time to move on." If you think this is an unlikely aftereffect of the fascinating but ugly goings-on in *What Ever*, bear in mind that appearances have kept intact from the same sorry fate the careers of others who managed their images *prettily*: Marilyn, Marlene, Greta, and Audrey among them.

Likely, the only saving grace in this debacle is that both actresses left behind two very fine performances in *Jane*, and the kind of sparring partnership that gives gay movie fans much to love. Here are five more:

Joan Crawford and Mercedes McCambridge
in *Johnny Guitar* (1953)

Bette Davis and Miriam Hopkins
in *Old Acquaintance* (1943)

Faye Dunaway and Estelle Parsons
in *Bonnie and Clyde* (1967)

Shirley MacLaine and Anne Bancroft
in *The Turning Point* (1977)

Elizabeth Taylor and Richard Burton
in *Who's Afraid of Virginia Woolf?* (1966)

By the way, who's the "babe" in Jane*?:*
The teenaged girl next door is actually Davis's daughter, B. D. Merrill, from her marriage to actor William Sherry.

"But cha ahhr, Blanche, ya ahhr in that chair!"

Above: Spoken nastily by Jane Hudson (Bette Davis) to remind her wheelchair-bound sister, Blanche Hudson (Joan Crawford), that she may forever be at her mercy. *Right:* Blanche and Jane look out of the bedroom window while discussing family matters. Kobal

1960. MGM. Directed by Henry Levin. Starring George Hamilton, Dolores Hart, Paula Prentiss, Jim Hutton, Yvette Mimieux, Connie Francis, Frank Gorshin, Barbara Nichols, and Chill Wills.

★

The basic story: Four college coeds, desperately needing a break from the Midwestern snow, pile into a car and venture south to the sandy beaches of Ft. Lauderdale, Florida, for a week of fun and sun.

★

About five minutes into *Boys* one of the comely coeds in a convertible, Tuggles (played by Paula Prentiss, whose long limbs and high-cheekboned hijinks made her an instant "gaydore"), announces to her fellow female travelers that they should all admit that the only reason for their trip to Ft. Lauderdale is to find men and get a tan. At that same exact moment, it should also become apparent why gay men are joining them on their ride.

By now it should also be pretty darn clear to readers that any movie that concerns itself mainly with the *miss*-adventures of women (and there are four fun ones in *Where*) is a safe bet to win gay male viewers. However, just because *Where* follows the fab-female-equals-gay-fan formula doesn't mean it hasn't put in a touch more spice here or added a new ingredient there. And coincidentally, since it is a similar film to another entry in the "girls-on-the-go" genre from the same time, *The Best of Everything* (1959), comparing the soubrettes is a good way to see differences in the soufflés. Both deal with the all-important "man-woman" dynamic, but *Where* cuts out the idle career chatter (heard in *Best*) and focuses,

rather openly, on interpersonal physical relationships, otherwise known as noncommittal sex, a subject that this silly-seeming comedy was talking about quite seriously. Somewhat revolutionary for its time, this discussion of sexual freedom is also part of the distinct queer charm of *Boys*, and one still in conversation because it cautions how too much playing around can have its consequences. And here you thought it was just about suntans and sand!

While we're thinking about bright beaches, *Where* also enjoys great gay benefits from its sunny location. When composer Neil Sedaka wrote the signature theme hit for "tomboyish" Connie Francis, it is likely that neither knew (but really, isn't that title alone so obvious?), nor did MGM (the producing studio), that Ft. Lauderdale would itself be cast as a star on the queer cultural scene. They even filmed part of it, of course unknowingly, in what would become a famous gay nightclub and hotel, the Marlin Beach. But it was and has remained a hotspot to go where the "boys" are ever since.

Five more films focused on where the "boys" like to go:

★

London in *Blow Up* (1966)
Palm Springs in *Palm Springs Weekend* (1963)
Rome in *Three Coins in the Fountain* (1954)
San Francisco in *Vertigo* (1958)
Venice in *Summertime* (1955)

"I'd rather die than go home with an uneven tan."

Above: Spoken by Tuggles Carpenter (Paula Prentiss) to her friends upon learning that because of low funds suntan lotion will have to be rationed. *Left:* Gathered on the crowded Ft. Lauderdale beach are Merritt Andrews (Dolores Hart) and her Brown University boyfriend Ryder Smith (George Hamilton), Tuggles and her college-educated escort TV Thompson (Jim Hutton). Everett

1939. MGM (AAN). Directed by Victor Fleming. Starring Judy Garland (AA, special), Frank Morgan, Ray Bolger, Jack Haley, Bert Lahr, Margaret Hamilton, Billie Burke, Charley Grapewin, and Clara Blandick.

★

The basic story: A young girl runs away to escape those whom she feels are unsympathetic, but is persuaded to return home by a traveling entertainer. Arriving back at the same time as a raging cyclone, an injury causes her to black out before she has a chance to find shelter.

★

Readers, *Fabulous!* can tell we are nearly at the close of our book-long journey, because it can see the end of the rainbow. (Hyuck.) Yes, almost everything about *Oz* is fodder for making fun, isn't it? And how cliché is including *Wizard* among the film favorites of gay men? Let's just hope this *Fabulous!* walk down the Yellow Brick Road will have something new to show those coming along for a stroll. Well, alrighty then.

All films are basically fantasies, but *Oz* is the best kind because it combines the ultimate trip (rainbow!) with the greatest reason for staying put ("There's no place like home"). But what is it about gay men that attracts them to fantasy in the first place? Is it because we feel real life mistreats us so much that these films provide necessary escape and protection? Possibly. (As the world opens to us—and it is, slowly—will this escapist need lessen? We'll see.) But the fantastic gay allure of *Oz* is not really why we walk down that fabled road. Arguably, it is the "homeward bound" message that connects most deeply with gay men——because so many do not feel connected. In that way *Oz* is not really

a fantasy at all (at least in the grandiose sense) but a wish-fulfillment film (in the humblest sense). All gay men dream of one day just feeling like there is some place to call home (knowing some might never have the option). Herein, gay viewers may have noticed something a tiny bit queer about *Oz* already. It seems that once our little gingham-clad ambler (Dorothy) finds herself back in her domicile she is surrounded by individuals whom most traditionalists would label as an "alternate" family. Readers, you did notice that already, didn't you?

Yes, queerly *Oz* is a place full of gayness every time you round a bend. For instance, take the Emerald City. Isn't it just a *verte* version of Manhattan, full of pretty people and a horse painted up in colors that change for the occasion? Like the "great and powerful" one himself, isn't the place just a fruity façade? And about that "wizard" trying to be someone special, with his outward bluster and pretentious intonation, all the while hoping no one will notice that he's not! And how about the demure demeanors of the "best friend" Scarecrow, the "sensitive" Tin Man, and the Cowardly Lion (especially when he's gets a lovely ribbon-in-the-hair touch)? *Fabulous!* won't even bother with the "sister-ishness" of spinster Almira Gulch or how the Wicked Witch (both fiendishly well played by Margaret Hamilton) always refers to Dorothy as "my pretty."

Heck, the gay edge Garland brings is almost superfluous. Almost. It does pull *Oz* back down to earth. Here was a woman who seemed never to find a happy home, but who brought much happiness to those who shared in her search. She is our melancholy reminder that finding it may not be such an easy road.

"My! People come and go so quickly here!"

Above: Spoken by a bewildered Dorothy Gale (Judy Garland) to the Munchkins of Munchkinland after Glinda, the Good Witch (Billie Burke), hurriedly departs. *Right:* Dorothy awakens in bed with her alternate family, including, from top left clockwise, Professor Marvel (Frank Morgan), Uncle Henry (Charley Grapewin), Zeke (Bert Lahr), Auntie Em (Clara Blandick), Hickory (Jack Haley), and Hunk (Ray Bolger). Everett

1939. MGM. Directed by George Cukor. Starring Norma Shearer, Joan Crawford, Rosalind Russell, Mary Boland, Paulette Goddard, Joan Fontaine, Lucile Watson, Phyllis Povah, Virginia Weidler, Ruth Hussey, Marjorie Main, and Hedda Hopper.

★

The basic story: A "friendly" group of talkative, well-to-do women discover that one among them, the most noble of the bunch, is being cheated upon by her husband with a cosmetics department salesgirl. The pair divorce, but soon come to realize that neither is happy with the new arrangements.

★

As troubling a thought as this might be to some (including the author!), if one had to winnow the list of *Fabulous!* films down from seventy-five to, say, ten, doing so wouldn't be as difficult as one might think. Instantly, *Eve* and *Oz* would be included, and, without a moment's hesitation, this little celluloid "cat-filled" catamaran, too. (The rest of the ten *Fabulous!* willingly leaves to your discretion.)

The simple reason why a film like *Women* is included in *Fabulous!*, long or short list, should be rather evident just by the title alone. But even if that isn't enough of a clue—or its cleverest of clever dialogue, that crazy fashion show (color-inserted at just the right moment)—and a quick read through of the cast credits is needed to seal the deal, further investigation into why this all-female film is *fabulously* featured is still necessary. Why? Although it might be fairly obvious why it is that *Women* is a gay male favorite, the fact that many real women don't share in our affinity for it might not

be—and the causes that separate us tell a little something about the current standings of both groups.

Directed by the "queen" of women's directors, George Cukor, *Women* is an at times too-glamorous-to-be-believed look at the oh-so-tortured-and-tumultuous lives of a group of too-rich-to-be-bothered "ladies" (and the word is used kindly)—plus one from the wrong side of the tracks. Now this is where things begin to go astray. When *Women* was released, Hollywood rightly believed audience members, especially the "fairer sex," loved to vicariously watch the travails of the rich. As time wore on, though, the class distinction that automatically made Crystal Allen the villainess of the piece just because she was a poor-and-lowly shopgirl wore thin on women (including playwright Clare Booth) who saw the rest of the supposedly civilized bunch as mainly manipulative backstabbers, independent so long as they had money from either their marriage to or divorce from wealthy husbands (which also renders the film strangely sexist).

Basically, all this has made *Women* unacceptable to watch for many modern females. But it is not enough of a deterrent for gay males. Yes, we are wholly aware of the film's lately political incorrectness, but can still allow that it is the march of time that has turned its once silly tone into something now viewed more seriously. Further, *Women* has enough ridiculously campy overtones to compensate for its trespasses into present-day out-of-bounds territory. Essentially, gay men are used to taking whatever pleasures they can from film along with the bad, for without this ability nearly 100 percent of all movies would be unwatchable. Heavens, then where would we be?

"There's a name for you ladies, but it isn't used in high society—outside of a kennel."

Above: Spoken frustratingly but pointedly by Crystal Allen (Joan Crawford) to all the ladies finally gathered in the powder room. *Left:* Edith Potter (Phyllis Povah) and Sylvia Fowler (Rosalind Russell) try to get the goods on shopgirl Crystal. Everett

Young Frankenstein

1974. Twentieth Century-Fox. Directed by Mel Brooks. Starring Gene Wilder, Marty Feldman, Madeline Kahn, Peter Boyle, Cloris Leachman, Teri Garr, Kenneth Mars, Gene Hackman, and Richard Haydn.

★

The basic story: A surgeon inherits the castle dwelling of his "mad" scientist grandfather. In this new home he finds the notes for his relative's reanimation experiments and reluctantly endeavors to re-create them.

★

This is the last of the seventy-five films in *Fabulous!* and rather odd in that it is not exactly the "gayest." Actually, far from it. But this is a bonus in terms of showing how gay men are not as restrictive about the types of films they like as some might think. However, while our attraction to a film like, say, *The Women* is unmistakable (or should be to anyone who's ever had a "gay" film conversation), that of *Young* can be too, but only with a little *queer*-ification.

This wildly popular comedy (a critical favorite, too) happens to be a "viewer's choice" for straight males. Why? Well, that is something for another book entirely (and one that *Fabulous!* can scarcely comprehend). But maybe this heterosexual attraction can be distilled down to one word: *goof.* Presumably, "goof" (as in "goofs on") is a more "guy" recognizable term than "spoof," and *Young* is a spot-on one of classic horror films—a category that both persuasions appreciate. However, while gay men love parody, when it is done well and is about a fave film genre, just because this is a clever one done on horror does not properly explain why our paths cross. But *Young* apes the creatures

from the black-and-white period of Universal Studios in the thirties (particularly James Whale's original and his soon-to-be "bride"), and this distinction makes all the difference. The *Young* take on a spiffy pair of spooky tales is the twist that ensnares us gay men. So there you have it (or, as is usual, part of it).

No doubt we would deign to give *Young* a second glance because of its mimicry of our favorite monsters. But this is not really why gay men care, and hardly enough to make it a *Fabulous!* seventy-five finalist. However, to those with gay intuition it would seem the cast of *Young* is clearly the spellbinder. But, while kudos are given to all the men for their *Young* work, it is at the laugh-inducing ladies we more fondly gaze—terrific Teri Garr (as *tit*-tering Inga), keen Cloris Leachman (as chalk-white Frau Blucher—*n-e-i-g-h!*), and an always marvelous Madeline Kahn (as ermine-wrapped Elizabeth). The presence of these three is part of a long queer tradition of needing funny females to make those things created by the "straight male" world tolerable, sometimes vastly enjoyable. In everything from television's *Saturday Night Live* to moviedom's bedroom comedies, it has almost always been the wiles of the women which separate the "nay" from the "yea" stack of gay celluloid choices. Now you know.

The seventy-five films of *Fabulous!* finish here with this note: Sometimes what makes a film special to us is almost indistinguishable (as it was here with *Young*). But just because something can't be seen, does that mean it isn't really there? Ask any gay man who's had to go looking and he'll probably answer no. *The End.*

"No tongues."

Above: Spoken by Elizabeth (Madeline Kahn) as kissing instructions to her fiancé, Dr. Fredrick Frankenstein (Gene Wilder). *Right:* Fredrick tries to convince Elizabeth that they can sleep together in his grandfather's castle. Kobal

Because gay men like to keep things as orderly, organized, and complete as possible, *Fabulous!* is including an additional twenty feature films and five TV films to make it an even hundred. Again, they are only suggestions to consider watching as part of the total "gay" movie experience.

★

Bambi (1942. Walt Disney). For those who believe that a boy's best friend is his mother, that fathers will come around eventually, and that as an adult skunk you can never expect to be anything more than a florist if they name you Flower.

★

Bell, Book and Candle (1958. Columbia. Directed by Richard Quine. Starring James Stewart, Kim Novak, and Jack Lemmon). Proof that witches and warlocks really do exist, and what a chic lot they are! Rumor also has it that this film may have begot one of our fave TV shows, *Bewitched*, too.

★

Charade (1963. Universal. Directed by Stanley Donen, Starring Cary Grant, Audrey Hepburn, and Walter Matthau). The most sprightly of the sixties spy spoofs (aka the "caper," quite the gay favorite category itself).

★

Cleopatra (1934. Paramount. Directed by Cecil B. DeMille. Starring Claudette Colbert, Henry Wilcoxon, and Warren William). A "milky" Colbert and a "daddy" Wilcoxon, in one of DeMille's most deliciously in de-Nile!

★

Death Becomes Her (1992. Universal. Directed by Robert Zemeckis. Starring Meryl Streep, Goldie Hawn, and Bruce Willis). One of the very, very few recent celluloid "catfights" of any laughing matter.

★

The Eyes of Laura Mars (1978. Columbia. Directed by Irvin Kerschner. Starring Faye Dunaway, Tommy Lee Jones, Brad Dourif, and Rene Auberjonois). Not even close to being as suspenseful as one would hope, but an absolute gay viewing and listening requirement just to see the fiery fashion shoots (Faye and Tommy aren't bad on the "eyes," either) and hear the "flaming" soundtrack.

★

Fargo (1996. Polygram [AAN]. Directed by Joel Coen [AAN]. Starring Frances McDormand [AA], William H. Macy [AAN], and Steve Buscemi). Evidence that "twisted" flicks can add us to their audience mix (and for bedroom-eyed Peter Stormare's sexy but sicko killer).

★

Grand Hotel (1932. MGM [AA]. Directed by Edmund Goulding. Starring Greta Garbo, John Barrymore, Lionel Barrymore, and Joan Crawford). The grandmother of all star-studded pictures, giving birth to the whole genre.

★

Hercules (1959. Dyaliscope [Italy]. Directed by Petro Fransisci. Starring Steve Reeves and Sylvia Koscina). The first in a whole array of gaily attractive dubbed films, thanks to lots of oily muscles and loincloths.

★

I'll Cry Tomorrow (1955. MGM. Directed by Daniel Mann. Starring Susan Hayward [AAN], Richard Conte, Jo Van Fleet, and Eddie Albert). The best fifties version of the "woman's picture," and a Hayward performance that can still make you cry today.

Magnificent Obsession (1954. Universal. Directed by Douglas Sirk. Starring Jane Wyman [AAN], Rock Hudson, and Agnes Moorehead). One of Sirk's finest and the film that hewed Rock into a star.

★

Moulin Rouge! (2001. Bazmark [AAN]. Directed by Baz Luhrmann. Starring Nicole Kidman [AAN], Ewan McGregor, Jim Broadbent, and John Leguizamo). Debatedly credited for kick-starting the movie musical back in business, it is a dazzling showpiece for a new auteur of immense "gay" sensibilities.

★

Mr. Skeffington (1944. Warner Bros. Directed by Vincent Sherman. Starring Bette Davis [AAN] and Claude Rains [AAN]). Bette at her vainest, most self-important—and "gayest"? Reader's choice.

★

The Opposite of Sex (1998. Sony. Directed by Don Roos. Starring Christina Ricci, Martin Donovan, and Lisa Kudrow). Probably one of the hardest of all the films in *Fabulous!* to classify—and that's a good thing! Is it a gay or straight dramedy? Watch and learn why it doesn't matter when the movie is good.

★

Pride and Prejudice (1940. MGM. Directed by Robert Z. Leonard. Starring Laurence Olivier, Greer Garson, and Edmund Gwenn). Literate and immensely likable comedy of manners, with those great gay favorites Garson (so classy!) and Olivier (what a chassis!).

★

Sophie's Choice (1982. Universal. Directed by Alan J. Pakula. Starring Meryl Streep [AA], Kevin Kline, and Peter

MacNicol). Not exactly a day in the park, but certainly a field day for Streep's dramatic-arts versatility (that accent!) and always our first choice from her dense résumé.

★

Sorry, Wrong Number (1948. Twentieth Century-Fox. Directed by Anatole Litvak. Starring Barbara Stanwyck [AAN], Burt Lancaster, and Ed Begley). Terror, the gay way: from inside the plush boudoir of a spoiled woman.

★

Tea and Sympathy (1956. MGM. Directed by Vincente Minnelli. Starring Deborah Kerr, John Kerr, and Leif Erickson). Even though it's underwhelming on many levels and has that classic cop-out ending, *Tea* is still a milquetoast milestone (but one begging to be redone).

★

Titanic (1953. Twentieth Century-Fox. Directed by Jean Negulesco. Starring Clifton Webb, Barbara Stanwyck, Robert Wagner, Audrey Dalton, Brian Aherne, and Thelma Ritter). One of the best comparisons *Fabulous!* can give for Hollywood productions then and overproductions now (and a chance to see Wagner as quite the young cutie!).

★

What's Up, Doc? (1972. Warner Bros. Directed by Peter Bogdanovich. Starring Barbra Streisand, Ryan O'Neal, Kenneth Mars, and Madeline Kahn). A seventies screwball comedy that's a queer winner with its attractive leads.

From the previous spread, left: Scene still of singer Lillian Roth (Susan Hayward) in the musical biopic *I'll Cry Tomorrow.* Everett. *Previous spread, right:* Publicity still of Kim Novak as the witch, Gillian Holroyd, holding Pyewacket the cat (and "familiar"), from *Bell, Book and Candle.* Everett. *This page, left:* Ryan O'Neal as Howard Bannister in *What's Up, Doc?* Everett

When it comes to books showcasing the "finest" in film, far too often the works of the small screen are excluded. However, that would never be the case in a collection of gay favorites, as many made-for-television films rank right up near the top. (The only time you shouldn't expect to see them is if the book has been put together by some hoity-toity hissy-fitter who felt the idea of including TV movies was beneath him. *Fabulous!* is hardly aiming that high, it just wants to have fun!) Admittedly, in order to properly include them one must use an amended set of criteria that allows for restrictive budgets, casts, and crews. Otherwise, comparing the two will always make the telefilm appear like the poorer cousin (and that isn't very nice). Fortunately, by using altered guidelines it becomes quickly apparent that the boob tube has produced a credible crop of celluloid classics, and while they may not be as richly relevant as those made for the big screen, they still give many a gay man "reel" pleasure, and here is the *Fabulous!* top five.

★

Alex, the Other Side of Dawn (1977. Directed by John Erman. Starring Leigh McCloskey, Eve Plumb, Juliet Mills, and Earl Holliman). All you need to know is that adorable Alex, searching for his girl Dawn in the big bad city, has no money and his only discernible talent is in wearing tight jeans (and what an asset that is!).

★

The Boy in the Plastic Bubble (1976. Directed by Randal Kleiser. Starring John Travolta, Robert Reed, and Diana Hyland). You mean they had Travolta sealed in a room, and they let him get out?

The Girl Most Likely To (1973. Directed by Lee Phillips. Starring Stockard Channing, Ed Asner, and Jim Backus). What's not for a gay man to love? A once "ugly duckling" gets cosmetic surgery and seeks revenge on those who mistreated her former self (and Joan Rivers helped write the teleplay!).

★

Trilogy of Terror (1975. Directed by Dan Curtis. Starring Karen Black, Robert Burton, and John Karlen). C'mon, a crazy, cross-eyed Karen as twins— one good, one bad—and a doll with a dagger?

★

A Woman Scorned: The Betty Broderick Story (1992. Directed by Dick Lowry. Starring Meredith Baxter, Stephen Collins, and Stephen Root). Based on the true story of a San Diego murder case about a woman who murders her ex-husband (and his girlfriend), *Scorned* is a one-eighty acting turn for Baxter, who played the loving mom on TV's long-running *Family Ties*, making this a too-twisted treat. (Catch the sequel, too: *Her Final Fury: Betty Broderick, the Last Chapter.*)

And, for readers to grow on, one last *Fabulous!* film:

For Ladies Only (1981. Directed by Mel Damski. Starring Gregory Harrison, Marc Singer, and Viveca Lindfors). Hunky Harrison as a struggling actor who must strip to make ends meet! Yeah, right, ladies only. (To the right, a publicity still of Harrison, as John Phillips, in *Ladies*. Please note that Mr. Harrison, a longtime gay male TV watcher's favorite, strips down in the picture to a black bikini marked with a "Z." Zowee!) Everett

Trivia Time!

When it comes to the subject of movies and lore, most gay men have such an impressive store of knowledge that it can amaze listeners how quickly Tinseltown trivia is answered. Unfortunately, to those with a tenuous hold on the topic a lack of expertise can become a painful source of humiliation, often resulting in a dearth of party invitations and the slinging of the two most hurtful of *homo*-insults: the threat of having your membership card revoked (although *Fabulous!* has yet to see an actual card) and being classified as a "bad" example of a gay person. Oh, the shame. Fortunately for those cinematically challenged sissies, *Fabulous!* has thought of an easy solution—ten movie questions to which every gay man *should* know the answers*—to help get the invites restarted and the barbs stopped until you are able to properly attend to this shortcoming with the help of a hard-core gay cinephile and a stack of DVDs.

★

1.) Who was originally cast then fired as Helen Lawson in *Valley of the Dolls*?

2.) Who was originally asked to play Mrs. Robinson in *The Graduate* but said "no" because it didn't fit her image?

3.) For what Bette Davis role was Claudette Colbert in preparation until injury forced her to bow out?

4.) Whom did MGM want to play Dorothy in *The Wizard of Oz* before settling on Judy Garland?

5.) For what role (and in what movie) has it been discussed that Marlene Dietrich richly deserved to win an Oscar but was not even nominated? (Bonus points if you know the generally accepted excuse why she was overlooked.)

6.) Who is Marni Nixon?

7.) Whose was the "voice" on the telephone speaking to Mia Farrow in *Rosemary's Baby*?

8.) Name one of three gay-fave and Oscar-winning Best Actresses who have appeared in three Best Picture winners. (Bonus points for naming the three films.)

9.) Name the only Oscar-winning Best Supporting Actor who has appeared in three Best Picture winners. (Bonus points for naming the three films.)

10.) Name the only actress who has won the quadruple crown of Oscar, Emmy, Tony, and Grammy. (Bonus points for naming the two actresses with disputed "crowns.")

★

Bonus questions (if you get these correct, you can classify yourself as a super cinequeer):

A.) Who is the "gongman"?

B.) Name the man who discovered and managed the careers of Rock Hudson and Tab Hunter, among others.

★

Special note: To any straight men who know the correct responses to the previous questions, *Fabulous!* salutes you with the title of "honorary" gay person. While this does not mean you are actually gay, *Fabulous!* suggests you not inform your mother, wife, or girlfriend of the results (unless you were waiting for a good reason to have "that" talk).

*All of which can be found on page 188.

Left: Anne Baxter (as Queen Nefretiri) and Charlton Heston (as Moses) in a scene still from *The Ten Commandments*. Everett. *This page:* Barbara Stanwyck (as Phyllis Dietrichson) stands behind the apartment door of her illicit partner (Fred MacMurray as Walter Neff) in *Double Indemnity*. Everett

And the Winner Is!

Guaranteed, once you get to talking movies with gay men, the subject of the Oscars will come up in conversation. For years the annual event has been inked onto our social calendar as indelibly as the Superbowl has for straight men. Incidentally, some people are actually inclined to think of the ceremony as the straight *female* version of the famed pigskin playoff. But we boys know better, don't we? However, ladies, you are always welcome at our home, where the party is sure to be perfect. But how does one give a great Oscar party? Well, lucky readers, *Fabulous!* is here to help with easy step-by-step instructions for giving the cinematic soiree of the season. (Just get your acceptance speech ready, because you'll be taking top honors yourself before the night is through!)

★

Step One: Where's the Party?

This must be decided way ahead of time, as many gay men like to play host and a conflict can easily occur. However, if this is a yearly event among pals, you can consider taking turns to be fair. Just remember, despite whose turn it may be it is always best to have as your final location the most urbane setting (a thirties Deco-decorated apartment is always nice), with ample seating and a *très* large, flat-screen television set for optimal viewing.

★

Step Two: Who to Invite?

Friends will always come first (and family, too, but only if they won't embarrass you). Yet the smart host will be sure to balance his guest list with an equal measure of those "in the know" (especially enough industry workers to make his "the" gathering) and others who can most benefit from being in the company of such wits and worldly creatures. Just be sure all invited guests plan on staying for the duration. Nothing says "pooper" faster than a party "poof" who leaves before the last award is given out. (Note: In this day and age of e-mails and instant messages, printed invitations are not always necessary. However, if you go the cyber route, it is still required that you gaily use your imagination and make your notifications as pretty as a picture.)

★

Step Three: What to Serve?

Because of the usual length of the show it will be necessary to feed guests. Properly done, comestibles should be served four ways: appetizers, an actual main course of sorts, sweets, and snacks. As insurmountable as this may already appear to some, it is actually quite easy to accomplish if you work with these simple suggestions: serve the food buffet style (table dining is out of the question unless you have monitors attached to every seat) and keep the menu to a minimum (but with enough variety to please the gourmands in the crowd—and they will be there). But how can one be sure to have the right menu items (along with chips and dip) for movieland's most starry night? Just look to the awards themselves for a place to start. Take the nominees for Best Picture in 2002 and use them as edible inspiration: *Chicago* brings to mind pizza (and yes, gay men will eat a pie on Oscar night); *The Hours* is rather eso-

"Hello gorgeous."

teric so you might end up with something with a clock motif (get it?); *The Pianist* was such a serious movie that you might want to leave it alone (if it hadn't been it could have been great fodder for a sparkling array of sophisticated "black-and-white" sweets or cocktails); *Gangs of New York* might have you searching the Internet for historic food ideas from the 1800s, but slackers could use it as the basis for that most basic of ingestibles: bread. Hopefully, by the time you reach *Lord of the Rings: The Twin Towers* you'll have a "gay" sense of this process, and something like fried onion rings will come to mind. Good boy! But wait! That would mean a *too* starchy food. And for a group of gay men? Never! Better to use the film's "forest" angle and mix up a green salad with, *maybe*, sliced circles of raw onion just to make the point obvious to those overwhelmed by the whole entertaining experience.

In addition, always have plenty of good-quality alcohol on hand (but use this time wisely to introduce the latest "gay" libation), discourage smoking unless you have a balcony or backyard, and try to find at least one thing to nosh on in the shape of Oscar himself (the ablest way to do this is to shop the most chi-chi food store or bakery in town—they are sure to have something apropos—but no more than a few days beforehand, lest the cookies go stale).

★

Step Four: What to Do?

Aside from watching the actual event, it is important to keep your easily bored guests occupied during long commercial breaks and memorial tributes (or else they'll begin to wander around your home and check in your closets—and you don't want that!). *Fabulous!* suggests that the handsome host(s) actively continue the commentary, no doubt begun at the beginning of the proceedings, on the presenters' and winners' attire, including their dress, jewelry, shoes, hairstyles, makeup, and latest romance or hired-for-the-night accompanying attendees (and always try engaging those neophytes new to the "scene" by asking their quaint opinion, which can be good for a derisive laugh or two).

Perhaps the most fun activity for those in attendance (other than watching and dishing) will be voting alongside the Academy. However, the only way to do this correctly is to give each person a ballot (one is downloadable right from the Academy's Web site—and won't that make you feel special?), a gold or silver pen or pencil, and five minutes to cast their votes—and add in a little wager to see which one of the "boys" really knows their movie stuff! (*Fabulous!* hint: If you really want to win, read every newspaper's and film magazine's "Oscar preview" issue and then only vote for movies you think will win, not the ones that should—there is a difference.)

★

Step Five: What to Wear?

Showing off a body kept in shape during the winter and as a preview of things to come in the summer months: gay friends can use this as a way to remind others that it may be time to get their tired butts to the gym. For emphasis, *Fabulous!* recommends dazzling them by wearing derriere-enhancing jeans and a tight silver or gold lamé stretch T-shirt that beautifully incorporates the "screen" or "winners" theme of the night just as a clever reminder.

"The winner is . . . Miss Vicki Lester!"

Above: Spoken by the previous year's Best Actor recipient, Nigel Peters (Richard Webb), to announce the fictional winner for the Best Actress Oscar in *A Star Is Born* (and the fictional film for which Lester won: *A World for Two*). *Left:* Just after the announcement, a still-seated Lester (Judy Garland) receives the applause of fans and her studio head, Oliver Niles (Charles Bickford). Kobal

Hopefully you enjoyed your journey through *Fabulous!*, one gay man's celebration of celluloid, and have found it fun and provocative, not foul and peevish. Remember, we all see things differently. This book's only intention was to try to show another point of view on these films. Thank you for joining in.

★

Many people have helped with *Fabulous!*, but the author would most like to thank his editor, Andrew Corbin, Joan Schadt, and everyone at Broadway who lent a hand; his agent, Christy Fletcher; as well as Liza Bolitzer, Jennifer Josephy, all the good people at Kobal, Glenn Bradie and the Everett Collection, and the best site on the web, the Internet Movie Database (IMDb). He would also like to thank his most *filmy* friends, Tony, Pat, Peter, Joyce, and Dan; also Jerry, John, and Joe, Mitch and Harris, Chris and Mike, Kevin and Alan, Darlene and John, Bob and Dave, Jim and Gary, Wayne and Kenny, and Dan O.; Red and all the fellas; and most especially Robert, for always sitting through these often unendurable endeavors through to the final reel.

The Answers.
From page 11: 1. Norma Desmond (Gloria Swanson) speaking in *Sunset Boulevard*.
From page 12: 2. Charlotte Vale (Bette Davis) speaking in *Now, Voyager*.
From page 15: 3. Lucy Lamont (Jean Hagen) speaking in *Singin' in the Rain*.
From page 16: 4. Daphne (Tony Curtis) speaking to Josephine (Jack Lemmon) in *Some Like It Hot*.
From page 20: 5. Norma Desmond again. 6. David Huxley (Cary Grant) speaking in *Bringing Up Baby* (1938).
From page 164: Singer Margaret Whiting (who was married to gay porn star Jack Wrangler!) and theater legend Ethel Merman.
From page 183: 1) Judy Garland; 2) Doris Day; 3) Margo Channing in *All About Eve*; 4) Shirley Temple; 5) for her "dual" roles in *Witness for the Prosecution* (1957) Dietrich was not exactly overlooked, but filmmakers, not wanting to spoil the "surprise" of the mystery, chose not to promote her double-sided performance; 6) Nixon is the woman who supplied the singing voice for Audrey Hepburn in *My Fair Lady*, Deborah Kerr in *The King and I* (1956), and Natalie Wood in *West Side Story* (1961); 7) Tony Curtis; 8) Diane Keaton in *The Godfather* (1972), *The Godfather, Part II* (1974), and *Annie Hall* (which won her the Best Actress award in 1977); Shirley MacLaine in *Around the World in Eighty Days* (1956), *The Apartment* (1960), and *Terms of Endearment* (which won her the Best Actress award in 1984); Meryl Streep in *Kramer vs. Kramer* (which won her the Best Supporting Actress award in 1979), *The Deer Hunter* (1980), and *Out of Africa* (1987) (Note: Streep won the Best Actress Award for *Sophie's Choice* in 1981); 9) Hugh Griffith in *Ben-Hur* (which won him the award in 1959), *Tom Jones* (1963), and *Oliver* (1968); 10) the only official competitive quad winner is Rita Moreno, who won the Oscar for *West Side Story*, an Emmy for *The Muppet Show* (1976) and for *The Rockford Files* (1977), the Tony for *The Ritz* (1975), and the Grammy for Best Children's Recording for "The Electric Company" (1972); the two disputed quad winners are Helen Hayes, who won two Oscars, as Best Actress for *The Sin of Madelon Claudet* (1931) and as Best Supporting Actress in *Airport* (1970), an Emmy in 1952, the Tony three times, and a disputed Grammy, because she was just an appearing artist, for Best Spoken Word Recording for *Great American Documents* (1976); and Barbra Streisand, who won the Oscar for *Funny Girl* (1968) and the Oscar as songwriter for "Evergreen" (1976), the Emmy three times, the Grammy six times, but was only given an honorary Tony in 1970. Bonus question answers: A) The "gongman" is the loincloth-clad hunk—first embodied in all his sweaty splendor by Bombardier Billy Wells—who opens the J. Arthur Rank Productions from England in the forties and fifties by, you guessed right, banging a gong. B) The notorious "gay" agent, Henry Willson, who is also credited with making stars out of Guy Madison and Rory Calhoun. Wow, don't those names look good on a résumé?!

This page: Publicity shot of Gloria Swanson as Norma Desmond from *Sunset Boulevard*. Everett. *Right:* Patty Duke as Neely O'Hara ranting in the infamous "pool scene" from *Valley of the Dolls*. Kobal

Index!

"A Pretty Girl Is Like a Melody," 159
Adam's Rib, 28, 29, 155
Adams, Dorothy, 103
Adams, Nick, *25,* 25, 128
Adelman, Herb, 44
Adlon, Percy, 43
Adventures of Priscilla, Queen of the Desert, 23, 100
Aherne, Brian, 47, 180
Aiello, Danny, 112
"Ain't There Anyone Here for Love?," 96
Airport, 30, 31
Albert, Eddie, 179
Albertson, Mabel, 44
Alda, Robert, 99
Alda, Rutanya, 111
Aldrich, Robert, 168
Alex, the Other Side of Dawn, 181
Alice in Wonderland, 80
All About Eve, 32, *33,* 123, 155, 175
All Quiet on the Western Front, 56
All This and Heaven Too, 108
Allbritton, Louise, 144
Allen, Lee, 88
Allen, Nancy, 64
Almodovar, Pedro, 104
American Gigolo, 160
American in Paris, An, 39, *158,* 159
Andersen, Bibi, 104
Anderson, Judith, *iv,* 103, 108, 156
Anderson, Kevin, 135
Anderson, Paul Thomas, 52
Andress, Ursula, 51
Andrews, Dana, *102,* 103
Andrews, Julie, 88, 119, 148, *149*
Andy Griffith Show, The, 139
Annie Get Your Gun, 155
Ann-Margret, 35, 67
Another Country, 23
Anthony Adverse, 75
Apartment for Peggy, 44
Apensanahkwat, 43
Arden, Eve, 108
Armstrong, Curtis, 135
Arnstein, Nick, 88
Around the World in Eighty Days, 116
Arquette, Patricia, 83
Arthur, 103
Arthur, Beatrice, 35
As Thousands Cheer, 159
Asner, Ed, 181
Asquith, Anthony, 39
Astaire, Fred, 159
Atencio, Xavier, 99
Auberjonois, Rene, 179
Aumont, Jean-Pierre, 107
Auntie Mame, 34, 35
Austen, Jane, 11, 68

Babe, 36, *37*
Baby Doll, 152
Bacall, Lauren, 96, *97,* 116, *117*
Backus, Jim, 181
Bad and the Beautiful, The, 38, 39
Bad Seed, The, 40, *41*
Bagdad Café, 42, 43
Baker, Carroll, 152
Baker, Diane, *46,* 47
Baker, Simon, 100
Bakke, Brenda, 100
Ball, Lucille, 35
Balsam, Martin, *54,* 55
Bambi, 179
Bancroft, Anne, 108, 168
Band Wagon, The, 159
Banderas, Antonio, 104, *105*
Banton, Travis, 143
Baranski, Christine, 67
Barbarella, 99
Bardem, Javier, 104
Barefoot in the Park, 44, *45*
Barker, Lex, 115
Barrie, Barbara, 56
Barrier, Edgar, 71

Barry, Dave, 147
Barry, Phillip, 127
Barrymore, John, 8, *9,* 75, 179
Barrymore, Lionel, 75, 179
Barton, Anne, 168
Bass, Saul, 99, 120
Bassermann, Albert, 132
Bates, Barbara, 32
Baxter, Anne, 32, *33,* 156, *182*
Baxter, Meredith, 181
Beaton, Cecil, 119
Beatty, Warren, 152
Beavers, Louise, 115
Bee Gees, the, 63
Beery, Wallace, 75
Begley, Ed, 144, 180
Bell, Jamie, 48, *49*
Bell, Book and Candle, 179, *179,* 180
Bellamy, Ralph, 139
Ben-Hur, 52
Bening, Annette, 72
Bennett, Bruce, 108
Bennett, Tony, 124
Berenson, Marisa, 60
Bergman, Ingrid, 79, 116, *117*
Berle, Milton, 124
Best, Edna, 91
Best of Everything, The, 1, 4, *5, 46,* 47, 171
Bewitched, 179
Bickford, Charles, 151
"Big Spender," 60
Bikel, Theodore, 119
Billy Elliot, 48, *49*
Binder, Maurice, 99
Bing, Herman, 80
Birdcage, The, 147
Birds, The, 50, 51
Bishop's Wife, The, 91
Bisset, Jacqueline, *30,* 31, 116, *117*
Black Narcissus, 132
Black, Karen, 181
Blackmer, Sidney, 139
Blackwell, Nicola, 48
Blackwell, Perry, 128
Blade Runner, 87
Blake, Amanda, 151
Blakely, Colin, 116
Blandick, Clara, 172, *173*
Bletcher, Billy, 80
Bloom, Orlando, 135
Blow Up, 171
Blyth, Ann, 108, *109*
Bochner, Hart, 56
Bogart, Humphrey, 79, 140
Bogdanovich, Peter, 180
Boland, Mary, 175
Bolger, Ray, 172, *173*
Bonham Carter, Helena, 136, *137*
Bonnie and Clyde, 168
Boogie Nights, 4, *7, 52,* 53
Boothe, Clare, 175
Borgnine, Ernest, 124
Born Yesterday, 155
Boy George, 104
Boy in the Plastic Bubble, The, 181
Boyd, Stephen (Steve), 47, 52, 124, *125*
Boyer, Charles, 44
Boyle, Peter, 176
Boys in the Band, The, 23
Box, John, 76
Brando, Jocelyn, 111
Brando, Marlon, 60, 152
Breakfast at Tiffany's, 54, 55, 140, 191, *192*
Breaking Away, 56, *57*
Brennan, Walter, 175
Brett, Jeremy, *118,* 119
Brice, Fanny, 88, 184
Brickman, Paul, 135
Bride of Frankenstein, The, 58, 59
Broadbent, Jim, 180
Broderick, Matthew, 84, 139
Bronson, Charles (Chuck), 52

Brook, Clive, *142,* 143
Brooks, Mel, 59, 176
Brooks, Richard, 71
Brophy, Edward, 80, 163
Brown, Joe E., 147
Brown, Julie, 68
Brown, Vanessa, 91, 92
Browne, Coral, 35
Brynner, Yul, 156, *157*
Buckley, Betty, 64
Bugs Bunny, 36
Bullock, Sandra, 84
Buono, Victor, 168
Burke, Billie, 75, 172
Burke, Paul, 164
Burton, Richard, 168
Burton, Robert, 181
Burton, Tim, 83
Buscemi, Steve, 179
Bush, George, Sr., 104
Bushman, Francis X., 140
Bye, Bye Birdie, 67
Byron, Lord (George Gordon), 59

Cabaret, 60, *61*
Cactus Flower, 88
Cage, Nicholas, 112, *113*
Caged, 155
Cahn, Sammy, 47
Cain, James, 108
Calamity Jane, 43
Calhoun, Monica, 43
Calhoun, Rory, 96
Call Me Madam, 67
"Calling You," 43
Callow, Simon, 136
Campbell, Jessica, 84
Can't Stop the Music, 62, 63
Capote, Truman, 55
Carmichael, Jim, 80
Caron, Leslie, *158,* 159
Carr, Allan, 63
Carr, Charmian, 148
Carradine, John, 156
Carrie, 64, *65*
Carroll, Janet, 135
Carroll, Leo G., *38,* 39, 120
Carson, Jack, 108, 151
Carter, (Jimmy), 63, 136
Cartwright, Angela, 148
Cartwright, Veronica, 51
Casablanca, 27, 79
Cass, Peggy, 35
Cassavetes, John, 139
Cassel, Jean-Pierre, 116, *117*
Cat on a Hot Tin Roof, 152
Catch Me If You Can, 99
Cavanaugh, Christine, 36
Chaney, Lon, Jr., 71
Channing, Stockard, 181
Chaplin, Geraldine, 76, *77*
Charade, 99
Chariots of Fire, 56
Chase, Duane, 148
Chase, Ilka, 123
Cheadle, Don, 52
Cher, 112, *113*
Cheung, Leslie, 147
Chicago, 26, 27, 60, *66,* 67, 184
Chicken Run, 36
Chiles, Lois, 167
Chinatown, 47
Christie, Julie, 76, *77, 190,* 191
Christopher, Dennis, 56, *57*
Cinderella, 155
Citizen Kane, 27
Clark, Fred, 35, 96, 155
Clarke, Gage, 40
Cleopatra (1934), 20, *21,* 179
Cleopatra (1963), 132
Clift, Montgomery, 92, *93,* 152, *153,* 155,
Clive, Colin, *58,* 59
Close, Glenn, 72, *73*

Clueless, 68, 69
Cobra Woman, 70, 71
Cockettes, The, 159
Coco, James, 103
Cocoon, 160
Coen, Joel, 179
Colbert, Claudette, 18, *21,* 179, 183
Collette, Toni, 95
Collier, Lois, 71
Collins, Joan, 71
Collins, Ray, 92
Collins, Stephen, 181
Come and Get It!, 75
Come Fly with Me, 31
Common Threads: Stories from the Quilt, 159
Connery, Sean, 52, 116, *117*
Conte, Richard, 179
Cooper, Gladys, 119, 123
Coote, Robert, 91
Coppola, Francis Ford, 60
Corby, Ellen, 140
Cotten, Joseph, 124
Coulouris, George, 116, *117*
Courtenay, Tom, 76
Crain, Jeanne, 32, 44
Crawford, Joan, 4, *5, 24,* 25, 47, 108, *109,* 168, *169,* *174,* 175, 179
Crosby, Bing, 159
Cromwell, James, 36, 100
Crowe, Russell, 100
Cruel Intentions, 72
Cruise, Tom, *134,* 135
Cukor, George, 28, 75, 119, 127, 151, 175
Curtis, Dan, 181
Curtis, Tony, 52, *146,* 147
Curtiz, Michael, 108
Cyrano de Bergerac, 155

da Silva, Howard, 111
DaCosta, Morton, 35
Daldry, Stephen, 48, 96
Dalio, Marcel, 128, 140
Dalton, Audrey, 180
Dalton, Phyllis, 76
Damski, Mel, 181
Dandridge, Dorothy 103
Danes, Claire, 95
Dangerous Liaisons, 72, *73*
Daniels, Jeff, 95
Danza, Tony, 144
D'Arcy, Alexander, 96
Darnell, Linda, 32
Dash, Stacey, 68
Davion, Alex, 164
Davis, Bette, 12, *13,* 32, *33, 122,* 140, 168, *169,* 180, 183
Davis, Geena, 160, *161*
Day, Doris, 67, 84, 128, *129*
Day-Lewis, Daniel, 136
Death Becomes Her, 18, 19, 179
DeCarlo, Yvonne, 156
Dee, Sandra, 99
de Havilland, Olivia, 92, *93*
De Mornay, Rebecca, 135
Deliverance, 19
Delon, Alain, 104
DeMille, Cecil B., *154,* 155, 156
Dench, Judi, 136
Dennis, Patrick, 35
Denny, Reginald, *114,* 115
DePalma, Brian, 64
DePatie-Freleng, 99
Depp, Johnny, *82,* 83, 135
Derek, John, 156, *157*
DeVito, Danny, 100
Deygas, Agnes, 99
"Diamonds Are a Girl's Best Friend," 96
Dickinson, Angie , 64
Diesel, Vin, 19
Dietrich, Marlene, 131, *142,* 143, 183
Diggs, Taye, 67
Dillane, Stephan, 95
Dillon, Bradford, 167

189

Dinner at Eight, 74, 75
Divine (Glenn Milstead), *130*, 131
"Do You Know Where You're Going To," 07
Doctor Zhivago, 76, *77*, *190*, 191
Donahue, Troy, 99
D'Onofrio, Vincent, 83
Donen, Stanley, 179
Donovan, Elisa, 68
Donovan, Martin, 180
Dooley, Paul, 56
Double Indemnity, 78, 79, *183*
Douglas, Kirk, 39
Douglas, Melvyn, 115
Douglass, Robyn, 56
Dourif, Brad, 179
Drake, Charles, 164
Draven, Jamie, 48
Dressed to Kill, 64
Dressler, Marie, 75
Dukakis, Olympia, 112
Duke, Patty, 164, *165*, 188, *189*
Dumbo, 80, *81*
Dunaway, Faye, *110*, 111, 168, 179

Earthquake, 116
Edwards, Blake, 55
Edwards, Cliff, 80
Edwards, Michael, 111
Elliot, Mike, 47
Election, 84, 85
Elliott, Denholm, 136
Elsom, Isobel, 91, 119
Emerson, Hope, 28
Emma, 68
Emperor's New Groove, The, 80
Erickson, Leif, 180
Erman, John, 181
Evans, Madge, 75
Evans, Maurice, 139
Evans, Robert, 47
Ewell, Tom, 28
Eyes of Laura Mars, The, 179

Faison, Donald, 68
Faithful, 112
Family Ties, 181
Fane, Billy, 48
Fantastic Voyage, 87
Farewell, My Concubine, 147
Fargo, 179, 191, *191*
Farrow, Mia, *138*, 139, 183
Fath, Jacques, 132
Father of the Bride, 39
Fawcett, Farrah, 87
Faylen, Frank, 88
Feld, Fritz, 44
Feldman, Marty, 176
Felton, Verna, 80
Field, Sally, 84, 95
Fight Club, 56
Findlater, John, 31
Finney, Albert, 116, *117*
Firth, Colin, 72
5,000 Fingers of Doctor T, The, 36
Fix, Paul, 40
Flagg, Darron, 43
Fleming, Victor, 172
Fletcher, Louise, 108
Flower Drum Song, 39
Fly, The, 86, 87
Foch, Nina, 107, 156
Fonda, Jane, 44, *45*
Fontaine, Joan, 175
For Ladies Only, 181, *181*
Forbidden Planet, 87
Ford, Harrison, 87
Forrest, Steve, 111
Forster, E. M., 136
Fosse, Bob, 60
Francis, Anne, 87, 88
Francis, Connie, 4, *6*, 171
Franco, James, 135

Fransisci, Petro, 179
Frears, Stephen, 72
Freeman, Kathleen, 87
Freemann, Mona, 92
From Russsia with Love, 52
Funny Face, 140
Funny Girl, 3, 4, 88, *89*, 184

Gabor, Zsa Zsa, 71
Gang's All Here, The, 71
Gangs of New York, 187
Garbo, Greta, 8, *9*, 179
Gardenia, Vincent, 112
Garland, Judy, 60, *150*, 151, 172, *173*, 183, *186*, 187
Garlington, May, 131
Garmes, Lee, 143
Garr, Teri, 176
Garson, Greer, *10*, 11, 180
Gavin, John, 99
Gentlemen Prefer Blondes, 96
Gerald McBoing Boing, 155
Gere, Richard, 67, 160
"Get Happy," 159
Ghost, 91
Ghost and Mrs. Muir, The, 90, 91
Gielgud, John, 103, 116
Gigi, 119
Gillette, Anita, 112
Givenchy, Hubert, 55, 140
Glen or Glenda?, 83
Goddard, Paulette, 175
Godfather, The, 60
Gods and Monsters, 23
Goldberg, Whoopi, 91
Golden Girls, The, 47
Goldwyn, Tony, 91
Gombell, Minna, 163
Gone With the Wind, 27
Gordon, Gavin, 59
Gordon, Michael, 128
Gordon, Ruth, 28, *138*, 139
Gordy, Berry, 107
Goring, Marius, 132, *133*
Gorshin, Frank, 171
Gosford Park, 116
Goulding, Edmund, 179
Goz, Harry, 111
Grable, Betty, 96, *97*
Graduate, The, 108, 183
Graham, Heather, 52
Grahame, Gloria, 39
Grand Hotel, 8, *9,* 179
Grant, Cary, 91, *114*, 115, *126*, 127, 147, 179
Grant, Lee, 164
Granville, Bonita, 123
Grapewin, Charley, 172, *173*
Graves, Rupert, 136
Grease, 63
Great Escape, The, 52
Great Expectations, 132
Great Ziegfeld, The, 159
Greim, Helmut, 60
Grey, Joel, 60
Grodin, Charles, 139, *186*, 187
Grimes, Tammy, 63
Group, The, 47
Guardian, The, 100
Guillén, Fernando, 104
Guinness, Alec, 76
Guttenberg, Steve, *62*, 63, 160
Guzman, Luis, 52
Gwenn, Edmund, 44, 180
Gyllenhaal, Jake, 84

Hackman, Gene, 176
Hagen, Jean, 28, 44
Hairspray, 131
Hale, Jean, 124
Haley, Jack, 172, *173*
Haley, Jack, Jr., 159
Haley, Jackie Earle, 56

Hall, Jon, 70, 71
Hall, Porter, 79, 163
Haller, Ernest, 108
Halliday, John, 127
Hamilton, George, *170*, 171
Hamilton, Margaret, 172
Hamilton, Murray, 167
Hammond, Nicholas, 148
Hampden, Walter, 140
Hans Christian Andersen, 132
Hanson, Curtis, 100
Hardwicke, Cedric, 156
Harlow, Jean, 74, 75
Harris, Ed, 95
Harrison, Gregory, 181, *181*
Harrison, Rex, 91, *118*, 119
Harron, Donald, 47
Hart, Dolores, 4, *6*, *170*, 171
Harvey, 91, 155
Hatosy, Shaun, 84
Havoc, June, 63
Hawn, Goldie, 19, 88, 179
Haydn, Richard, 144, 148, 176
Hayes, Helen, 31
Hayward, Susan, 164, *178*, 179, 180
Haywood, Jean, 48
Head, Edith, 124, 140
Heather, Jean, 79
Heckart, Eileen, 40
Heckerling, Amy, 68
Hedaya, Dan, 68
Hedison, David, 87
Hedren, Tippi, *50*, 51
Heflin, Van, 31
Hefti, Neal, 44
Heiress, The, 92, 93
Hello Frisco, Hello, 43
Helpmann, Robert, 132
Henreid, Paul, *122*, 123
Henry, Emmaline, 139
Henry, William, 163
Hepburn, Audrey, *54*, 55, 88, *118*, 119, 140, *141*, 179, 191, *192*
Hepburn, Katharine, 28, *29*, *126*, 127, 152, *153*, 184
Her Final Fury: Betty Broderick, the Last Chapter, 181
Hercules, 179
Herrmann, Bernard, 91, 120
Hersholt, Jean, 75
Heston, Charlton (Chuck), 52, 156, *157*, *182*
Hickman, Darryl, *14*, 15
Hiller, Wendy, 116, *117*, 119
Hinds, Samuel S., 71
Hitchcock, Alfred, 51, 120
Hobel, Mara, *110*, 111
Hobson, Valerie, 59
Hoffman, Dustin, 147
Hoffman, Philip Seymour, 52
Holden, William, 44, 140, *141*, 155
Holland, John, 119
Holliday, Judy, 28
Holliman, Earl, 180
Holloway, Stanley, 119
Holloway, Sterling, 80
Holm, Celeste, 32
"Honeysuckle Rose," 159
Hopkins, Miriam, 92, 168
Hopper, Hedda, 155, 175
Hopper, William, 40
Horne, Victoria, 91
Hotel, 31
Hours, The, 94, 95, 184
How to Marry a Millionaire, 96, *97*
Howard, John, 127
Howard, Leslie, 119
Huber, Harold, 163
Hudson, Rock, *25*, 25, 128, *129*, 180, 183
Hunter, Ross, 128
Hunter, Tab, 84, *130*, 131, 183
Hussey, Ruth, *126*, 127, 175
Huston, John, 76
Hutton, Jim, *170*, 171
Hyde-White, Wilfred, *118*, 119

Hyer, Martha, 47, 140
Hyland, Diana, 181

I Was a Male War Bride, 147
"I Wish I Didn't Love You So," 43
Ice Age, 36
"I'll Build My Own Tree," 164
I'll Cry Tomorrow, 178, 179, 180
Imitation of Life, 98, 99
Importance of Being Earnest, The, 39
Irving, Amy, 64
Ivory, James, 136

Jackson, Mahailia, 99
James Dean, 135
James, Henry, 92
Jane, Thomas, 52
Janney, Alison, 95
Jarré, Maurice, 76
Jenner, Bruce, *62*, 63
Jewison, Norman, 112
Jezebel, 123
Johnny Guitar, 168
Jones, Chuck, 36
Jones, Henry, 40
Jones, Jeffrey, 83
Jones, Shirley, 67
Jones, Tommy Lee, 179
Jourdan, Louis, 47

Kahn, Madeline, 176, *177*, 180
Kanin, Garson, 28
Karath, Kym, 148, *149*
Karlen, John, 181
Karloff, Boris, *58*, 59
Katt, William, 64, *65*
Kaufmann, Christine, 43
Kaye, Danny, 132
Keitel, Harvey, 160
Kelly, Gene, *158*, 159
Kelly, Nancy, 40, *41*
Kelly, Patsy, 139
Kelly, Paula, 60
Kennedy, George, 31
Kerr, Deborah, 15, 180
Kerr, John, *14*, 15, 180
Kerschner, Irvin, 179
Kidman, Nicole, 94, 95, 139, 180
Killing of Sister George, The, 35
King, Ken, 131
Kiss Me Kate, 67
Klein, Chris, 84, *85*
Klein, Kevin, 180
Kleiser, Randal, 181
Knight, Esmond, 132
Knowles, Patric, 35
Kohner, Susan, *98*, 99
Koscina, Sylvia, 179
Koster, Henry, 39
Kroc, Ray, 35
Kudrow, Lisa, 180
Kurtz, Swoosie, 72

L. A. Confidential, 100, *101*
Lady Sings the Blues, 88
Lahr, Bert, 172, *173*
Lamarr, Hedy, 71
Lancaster, Burt, 23, 31, 180
Lanchester, Elsa, *58*, 59
Landau, Martin, 83, 120
Landis, Jesse Royce, 120
Lane, Nathan, 147
Lang, Charles, 91
Lang, Doreen, 51
Lang, Walter, 144
Lange, Hope, 4, *5*, *46*, 47,
Lansbury, Angela, 108
"Last Dance," 43
Laughton, Charles, 59
Laura, 102, 103
Laurel (Stan) and Hardy (Oliver), 131
Laurie, Piper, 64
Law of Desire (La Ley del Deseo), 104, *105*

Lawford, Peter, 159
Lawrence of Arabia, 19
Leachman, Cloris, 176
Lean, David, 76
Lee, Anna, 91, 148, 168
Legally Blonde, 135
Leguizamo, Jim, 180
Lehman, Ernest, 120
Leigh, Vivien, 152
Lemmon, Jack, *146*, 147, 179
Lenya, Lotte, 152
Leonard, Robert Z., 180
Lerner, (Alan Jay) and Loewe, (Frederick), 119
Leto, Jared, 135
Letter, The, 123
Letter to Three Wives, A, 32
Levin, Henry, 171
Levin, Ira, 139
Lewis, Gary, 48
Leyton, John, 52
"Liberation," 63
Lili, 39
Liljan, John, 156
Lindfors, Viveca, 167, 181
Linley, Betty, 92
Lion in Winter, The, 184
Lion King, The, 80
Little Foxes, 123
Little Me, 35
Litvak, Anatole, 180
Liu, Lucy, 67
Loder, John, 123
Logan, Joshua, 76
Logan's Run, 87
Longtime Companion, 23
Lord of the Rings: The Twin Towers, 187
Lost Boys, The, 56
Louise, Tina, 139
Lowe, Edmund, 75
Lowry, Dick, 181
Loy, Myrna, *114*, 115, *162*, 163
Lubitsch, Ernst, 39
Luft, Sid, 151
Luhrmann, Baz, 67, 180
Lumet, Sidney, 116
Lynley, Carol, 31
Lyon, Sue, 35

MacDougall, Ranald, 108
MacGuire, Tobey, 135
MacLaine, Shirley, 168
MacMurray, Fred, *78*, 79, 183
MacNichol, Peter, 180
Mackie, Bob, 112
Macy, William H., 52, 179
Madame Bovary, 39
Madison, Guy, 52
Madsen, Micahel, 160
Magnificent Ambersons, The, 76
Magnificent Obsession, The, 16, *17*, 180
Mahogany, 106, 107
Mahoney, John, 112
Main, Marjorie, 44, 175
Malkovich, John, 72
Mame, 35
"Man That Got Away, The," 151
Man Who Came to Dinner, The, 144
Manchurian Candidate, The, 108
Mancini, Henry, 55
Mankiewicz, Joseph, 32, 91, 152, 156
Mann, Daniel, 179
Mann, Danny, 36
Mansfield, Jayne, 71
Marais, Jean, 104
Margolyes, Miriam, 36
Marie, Lisa, 83
Marlow, Lucy, 151
Marlowe, Hugh, 151
Mars, Kenneth, 176, 180
Marshall, Connie, 115
Marshall, Herbert, 87
Marshall, Rob, 67

Martin, Dean, *30*, 31
Martin, Steve, 11
Martinez, Nacho, 104
Martinez, Olivier, 104
Mary Poppins, 88
Mask, 112
Mason, James, 120, *121*, *150*, 151
Massey, Daniel, 103
Massey, Edith, 131
Massine, Léonide, 132
Mastroainni, Marcello, 104
Masur, Richard, 135
Mathis, Johnny, 47
Matthau, Walter, 179
Maupin, Armistead, 112
Maura, Carmen, 104
Maurice (film), 23
Maurice (novel), 136
McCambridge, Mercedes, 152, 168
McCloskey, Leigh, 181
McCormack, Patty, 40, *41*
McCoy, Matt, 100
McDonald, Christopher, 96
McDormand, Frances, 179, *191*
McGiver, John, 55
McGregor, Ewan, 180
McKellan, Ian, 144
McKenna, Siobhan, 76
McQueen, Butterfly, 25, 108
Meade, Julia, 128
Medford, Kay, 88
"Mein Herr," 60
Mell, Marisa, 107
Menzies, Heathe, 148
Merchant, (Ismai), 136
Merman, Ethel, 66
Merrill, B. D., 168
Merrill, Gary, 32
Meyer, Breckin, 68
Midler, Bette, 88
Midnight Express, 19
Mildred Pierce, 108, *109*, 111
"Milkshake," 63
Miller, Ann, 67
Mills, Juliet, 181
Milner, Martin, 164
Mimieux, Yvette, 4, *6*, 171
Min and Bill, 75
Mink Stole, 131
Minnelli, Liza, 60, *61*
Minnelli, Vincente, 39, 60, 180
Miranda, Carmen, 71
Mr. Blandings Builds His Dream House, *114*, 115
Mr. Skeffington, 13, 180
Mrs. Doubtfire, 147
Mitchell, Cameron, 96
Moffett, Sharyn, 115
Mohr, Gerald, 88
Molina, Alfred, 52
Molina, Miguel, 104
Mommie Dearest, *110*, 111
Monroe, Marilyn, 32, *33*, 96, *97*, 147
Montez, Maria, *70*, 71
Montgomery, Robert (Bob), 52
"Moon River," 55
Moonstruck, 112, *113*
Moore, Juanita, *98*, 99
Moore, Julianne, 52, 95
Moorehead, Agnes, 16, *17*, 180
Moorhead, Natalie, 163
Morali, Jacques, 63
Morgan, Frank, 172, *173*
Morse, Robert, 84
Murder on the Orient Express, 116, *117*
Moulin Rouge (1952), 76
Moulin Rouge! (2001), 67, 180
Muppet Movie, The, 36
Muriel's Wedding, 95
Murphy, Brittany, 68
Murray, Bill, 83
Music Man, The, 67
My Beautiful Laundrette, 23
My Fair Lady, *118*, 119, 140

"My Man," 88

Nash, Mary, 71, 127
Natwick, Mildred, 44, 72
Neal, Patricia, 55
Negulesco, Jean, 44, 96, 180
Neumann, Kurt, 87
New Yorker, 139
Newman, Alfred, 47
Newman, Paul, 152
Nicholas and Alexandra, 132
Nichols, Barbara, 171
Nightmare on Elm Street, 83
Ninotchka, 39
Nixon, Marni, 148, 183
Noonan, Chris, 36
Noonan, Tommy, 151
Norma Rae, 95
North by Northwest, 120, *121*
Novak, Kim, 179, *179*, 180
Now, Voyager, *122*, 123

Oberon, Merle, 31
O'Brian, Hugh, 31
O'Brien, Pat, 147
O'Connor, Donald, 159
O'Connor, Una, 59
O'Donnell, Chris, 84
O'Hara, Maureen, 144, *145*
O'Herlihy, Dan, 99
O'Neal, Ryan, *180*, 180
O'Neal, Patrick, 167
O'Neil, Barbara, 108
O'Sullivan, Maureen, 163
Odd Couple, The, 43
Oland, Warner, 143
Old Acquaintance, 168
Oliver!, 76
Olivier, Laurence (Larry), *10*, 11, 52, 180
Olson, Nancy, 155
One Flew Over the Cuckoo's Nest, 108
Only When I Laugh, 103
Opposite Sex, The, 71
Opposite of Sex, The, 180
Orry-Kelly, 35
Oscar, The, 124, *125*
Owens, Patricia, *86*, 87

Page, Geraldine, 152
Paget, Debra, 156, *157*
Paiva, Nestor, 115
Pajama Game, The, 67
Pakula, Alan J., 180
Palance, Jack, 43
Palette, Eugene, 143
Palm Springs Weekend, 171
Paltrow, Gwyneth, 68
Pangborn, Franklin, 123
Pantaliano, Joe, 135
Paragraph 175, 159
Parent Trap, The, 99
Paris Is Burning, 159
Parker, Eleanor, 124, *125*, 148
Parker, Sarah Jessica, *82*, 83
Parker, Suzy, 4, *5*, *46*, 47
Parkins, Barbara, 164
Parsons, Estelle, 168
Parting Glances, 23
Patrick, Lee, 108, 123, 128
Payne, Alexander, 84
Pearce, Guy, 100, *101*
Pee-wee's Big Adventure, 83
Pendleton, Nat, 163
Pepe, 116
Peppard, George, *54*, 55
Perils of Pauline, The, 43
Perkins, Anthony, 107, 116, *117*
Perrine, Valerie, *62*, 63
Perry, Frank, 111
Persoff, Nehemiah, 147
Peter Pan, 80
Peterson, Dorothy, 12, *13*
Peyton Place, 103

Pfeiffer, Michelle, 72
Philadelphia Story, The, *126*, 127
Phillippe, Ryan, 72
Phillips, Lee, 181
Pianist, The, 187
Pidgeon, Walter, *38*, 39, 88
Pillow Talk, 25, *25*, 128, *129*
Pinchot, Bronson, 135
Pink Flamingos, 131
Pink Panther, The, 99
Pirates of the Caribbean, 135
Pitt, Brad, 15, 135, 160, *161*
Place in the Sun, A, 76
Pleshette, Suzanne, 51
Plumb, Eve, 181
Plummer, Chrisopher, 148
Pointer, Priscilla, 64, 111
Polanski, Roman, 139
Pollack, Sydney, 167
Polyester, *130*, 131
Poncela, Eusebio, 104
Portrait of Jennie, 91
Poseidon Adventure, The, 31
Postman Always Rings Twice, The, 108
Potter, H. C., 115
Pounder, C.C.H., *42*, 43
Povah, Phyllis, *174*, 175
Powell, Dick, 39
Powell, Michael, 132
Powell, William, 96, *162*, 163
Powers, Tom, 79
Prefontaine, 135
Preminger, Otto, 103
Prentiss, Paula, 4, *6*, 139, *170*, 171
Pressburger, Emeric, 132
Preston, Robert, 103
Price, Vincent, 35, 87, 103, 156, *157*
Prick Up Your Ears, 72
Pride and Prejudice, *10*, 11, 180
Pryor, Nicholas, 135
Pucci, 139
Pygmalion, 119

Quaid, Dennis, 56, 160
Queen Latifah, 67
Queen of Outer Space, The, 71
Questal, May, 88
Quick and the Dead, The, 168
Quilley, Denis, 116, *117*
Quine, Richard, 179

Raft, George, 147
Rains, Claude, 79, 123, 180
Raksin, (David), 103
Randall, Tony, 128
Rapper, Irving, 123
Ratoff, Gregory, 32
Rebecca, 4, 108, 120
Red Shoes, The, 132, *133*
Redford, Robert, 44, 45, *166*, 167
Redgrave, Vanessa, 116, *117*
Reed, Alan, 55
Reed, Sir Carol, 76
Reed, Robert, 181
Reeves, Keanu, 72, 135
Reeves, Steve, 179
Reilly, John C., 52, 67, 95
Restoration, 132
Reynolds, Burt, 52, *53*
Reynolds, Debbie, 159
Ricci, Christina, 180
"Rich Man's Frug," 60
Richards, Beau, 107
Richardson, Miranda, 95
Richardson, Ralph, 76, 92
Rifkin, Ron, 100
Risky Business, *134*, 135
Ritter, Thelma, 32, 128, 180
Rivera, Chita, 60
Rivers, Joan, 181
Robards, Jason, 115
Roberts, Rachel, 116, *117*
Robinson, Edward G., 79, 156

191

This spread, left: Julie Christie as Lara getting ready to shoot Rod Steiger (Komarovsky) in the Christmas party scene from *Doctor Zhivago*. Everett. *Below:* Frances McDormand as Officer Marge Gunderson, her Oscar-winning role in *Fargo*, readying to shoot suspect Gaear Grimsrud (Peter Stormare). Kobal. *Closing page:* Audrey Hepburn in a famed publicity shot for *Breakfast at Tiffany's*. Kobal

Index!

Robson, Mark, 164
Roland, Gilbert, *38*, 39
"Roly Poly," 128
Roman Holiday, 88, 140
Roman Spring of Mrs. Stone, The, 152
Romeo and Juliet, 160
Romero, Cesar, 163
Room with a View, A, 136, *137*
Rooney, Mickey, 55, 159
Roos, Don, 180
Rope, 120
Rose, The, 88
Rosemary's Baby, *138*, 139, 183
Ross, Diana, 88, *106*, 107
Ross, Herbert, 88
Ross, Katharine, 139
Rouse, Russell, 124
Rovello, Jack, 95
Rudd, Paul, 68, 69
Rudin, Paul, 139
Rush, Barbara, 16, *17*
Russell, Jane, 96
Russell, Rosalind, *24*, 25, *34*, 35, *174*, 175
Russo, Jodean, 31
Rutherford, Margaret, 44

Sabu, 71
Sägebrecht, Marianne, *42*, 43
Sabrina, 140, *141*
Saint, Eva Marie, 120, *121*
St. John, Jill, 124
Saks, Gene, 44
Sales, Richard, 124
Samson, David, 131
Samson and Delilah, 155
Sand, Paul, 63
Sanders, George, 32, *33*, 40, 91
Sands, Julian, 136, *137*
Sarandon, Susan, 15, 160
Sassoon, Vidal, 139
Saturday Night Fever, 160
Saturday Night Live, 176
Scarwid, Diana, 111
Schwarzenegger, Arnold, 72, 136
Scott, Martha, 156
Scott, Ridley, 160
Scott, Zachary, 108
Scotti, Tony, 164
Seaton, George, 31
Seberg, Jean, 31, 103
"Secret Love," 43
Secret Storm, 111
Separate Tables, 116
Sex and the City, 47
Shanghai Express, *142*, 143
Shannon, Harry, 115
Sharif, Omar, 76, *77*, 88, *89*
Sharpsteen, Ben, 80
Shaw, George Bernard, 119
Shaw, Robert (Bob), 52
Shawlee, Joan, 147
Shearer, Moira, 132, *133*
Shearer, Norma, 175
Shelley, Mary, 59
Shelley, Percy, 59
Sherman, Vincent, 180
Sherry, William, 168
Sidney, George, 39
Sidney, Sylvia, 83
Silverstone, Alicia, 68, *69*
Simon, Neil, 44
Sinatra, Frank, 159
Since You Went Away, 52
Singer, Marc, 181
Singin' in the Rain, 44
Siodmak, Robert, 71
Sirk, Douglas, 99, 179
Sisto, Jeremy, 68
Sitting Pretty, 144, *145*
Smith, Maggie, 136
Smith, Roger, 35
Snipes, (Wesley), 131
Snow White, 80

Soles, P.J., 64
Some Like It Hot, 131, *146*, 147
Sommer, Elke, 51, 124
Sondergaard, Gale, 75
Sophie's Choice, 180
Sorry, Wrong Number, 22, 23, 180
Sothern, Ann, 32
Sound of Music, The, 63, 148, *149*
Spacek, Sissy, *64*, *65*
Spacey, Kevin, 100
Spartacus, 52
Spiderman, 20
Spradlin, G. D., 83
Stallone, Sylvester, 72, 136
Stanwyck, Barbara, *22*, 23, *78*, 79, 180, *183*
Stapleton, Maureen, 31
Star!, 103
Star Is Born, A, 150, 151, *186*, 187
Stern, Daniel, 56
Sting, The, 56
Steele, George "The Animal," 83
Steiger, Rod, 76, 191
Steiner, Max, 108, 123
Stevens, George, 76
Stevens, Naomi, 164
Stewart, Elaine, 39
Stewart, James, *126*, 127, 159, 179
Stewart, Paul, *38*, 39
Stone, Sharon, 168
Stormare, Peter, 179, 192
Straithairn, David, 100
Strangers on a Train, 120
Streep, Meryl, *18*, 19, 95, 140, 179, 180
Streetcar Named Desire, A, 152
Streisand, Barbra, *iii*, 88, *89*, *166*, 167, 180, 184, *185*
Suddenly, Last Summer, *1*, 4, 152, *153*,
Sullivan, Barry, 39
Sum of Us, The, 100
Summer Stock, 159
Summers, Hope, 139
Summertime, 171
Sunset Boulevard, *154*, 155, *188*, 188
Suspect, 160
Swanson, Gloria, *154*, 155, *188*, 188
Swayze, (Patrick), 131
Sweet Bird of Youth, 152
Sweet Charity, 60
Szubanski, Magda, 36

Tales of the City, 112
Tamblyn, Russ, 103
Tandy, Jessica, 51
Tanner, Edward Everett, III, 35
Tate, Sharon, 164
Taylor, Elizabeth, 11, 152, *153*, 159, 168
Taylor, Rod, 31, 51
Tcherina, Ludmilla, 132
Tea and Sympathy, *14*, 15, 180
Ten Commandments, The, 156, *157*, *182*, 183
Thank God It's Friday, 43
That's Entertainment, *158*, 159
Thelma and Louise, 15, 160, *161*
Thesiger, Ernest, *58*, 59
"They Can't Take That Away from Me," 159
Thin Man, The, *162*, 163
Three Coins in the Fountain, 171
Thurman, Uma, 72
Tierney, Gene, *90*, 91, *102*, 103
Tilly, Meg, 72,
Time, 139
Times of Harvey Milk, The, 159
Titanic (1953), 180
To Wong Foo, Thanks for Everything! Julie Newmar, 131
Tootsie, 147
Toy Story 2, 43
Tracy, Lee, 75
Tracy, Spencer, 28, *29*
Travolta, John, 63, 64, 160, 181
Trigere, (Pauline), 55
Trilogy of Terror, 181
Tucker, Forrest, 35
Turner, Debbie, 148
Turner, Lana, *38*, 39, 99, 100

Turning Point, The, 168
Tushingham, Rita, 76

Uninvited, The, 91

Valley of the Dolls, *1*, 4, 47, 164, *165*, 183, 188, *189*
Valmont, 72
Van Dyke, W. S., 163
Van Fleet, Jo, 179
Varden, Evelyn, 40
Velasco, Manuela, 104
Vertigo, 171
Victim, 23
Victor/Victoria, 103
Vilanch, Bruce, 107
Village of the Damned, 40
Village People, The (Alex Briley, David Hodo, Glenn Hughes, Randy Jones, Felipe Rose, Ray Simpson), *62*, 63
Villalonga, 55
Vincent, Jan-Michael, 84
Viva Las Vegas, 39
Vohs, Joan, 140
Von Sternberg, Josef, 131, 143
von Stroheim, Erich, 155

Wadsworth, Henry, *162*, 163
Wagner, Robert, 180
Walbrook, Anton, 132, *133*
Wahlberg, Mark, 4, *7*, 52, *53*
Walk on the Wild Side, 99
Walker, Justin, 68
Walker, Nancy, 63
Walters, Charles, 39
Walters, Julie, 48
Walton, Douglas, 59
War Games, 84
Warner, H. B., 156
Washbourne, Mona, 119
Washington Square, 92
Waters, John, 131
Watson, Lucille, 175
Way We Were, The, *166*, 167
Wayne, David, 28, *29*, 96
Wedding Banquet, The, 23
Weaving, Hugo, 36
Webb, Clifton, 103, 144, *145*, 180
Webb, Jack, 155
Webb, Richard, 187
Weidler, Virginia, 127, 175
Welch, Raquel, 87
Welles, Orson, 76
Wells, Stewart, 48
Wepper, Fritz, 60
Whale, James, 59, 176
What Ever Happened to Baby Jane?, 168, *169*
What's Up, Doc?, *180*, 180
"When She Loved Me," 43
When Worlds Collide, 87
Where the Boys Are, 4, *6*, *170*, 171
White, Jesse, 40
White, Joni Ruth, 131
White Cargo, 71
Whiting, Leonard, 160
Whitney, Dorothy, 55
Who's Afraid of Virginia Woolf?, 168
Wickes, Mary, 123
Widmark, Richard, 116
Wilcoxon, Henry, 20, *21*, 156, 179
Wilder, Billy, 79, 140, 147, 155, 156
Wilder, Gene, 176, *177*
Williams, Billy Dee, 107
Williams, John, 140
Williams, Robin, 147
Williams, Tennessee, 152
Williams, Warren, 179
Willis, Bruce, 179
Wills, Chill, 171
Willy Wonka and the Chocolate Factory, 36
Wilson, Luke, 135
Winters, Shelley, 31
Wise, Robert, 148
Witherspoon, Reese, 72, 84, *85*
Wizard of Oz, The, *2*, 4, 32, 159, 172, *173*, 175, 183

Wolfe, Ian, 115
Woman Scorned: The Betty Broderick Story, A, 181
Women, The, *24*, 25, *174*, 175
Wonder Boys, 135
Wong, Anna May, 143
Wood, Natalie, 91
Wood, Peggy, 148
Woolley, Monty, 144
Wyburd, Sophie, *94*, 95
Wyman, Jane, 16, *17*, 180
Wyler, William, 88, 92

"YMCA," 63
Yates, Peter, 56
York, Michael, 60, 116, *117*
"You'll Never Know," 43
Young Frankenstein, 59, *176*, 177
Young, Bruce A., 135
Young, Freddie, 76
Young, Robert, 144
Young, Roland, 127

Zellweger, Renee, *26*, 27, *66*, 67
Zemeckis, Robert, 179
Zeta-Jones, Catherine, *26*, 27, 67